THE
MASTER-KEY
TO RICHES

Also by Napoleon Hill
Published by Fawcett Columbine:

GROW RICH! WITH PEACE OF MIND

THINK AND GROW RICH

YOU CAN WORK YOUR OWN MIRACLES

The Master-Key to Riches

Napoleon Hill

Fawcett Columbine • New York

A Fawcett Columbine Book
Published by Ballantine Books

http://www.randomhouse.com

Library of Congress Catalog Card Number: 97-90490

ISBN: 0-449-00111-3

Manufactured in the United States of America

First Fawcett Crest Edition: November 1965
First Ballantine Books Mass Market Edition: July 1982
First Ballantine Books Trade Edition: August 1997
10 9 8 7 6 5 4 3 2 1

Contents

Page

THE MASTER-KEY TO RICHES

Foreword

"I give and bequeath to the American people the greater part of my vast fortune, which consists of the philosophy of individual achievement, through which all of my riches were accumulated . . ."

Thus began the last will and testament of Andrew Carnegie. It is the prologue of a story which may well mark the most important turning-point in the lives of all who read it.

The story began in the late Fall of 1908, when Andrew Carnegie called me in, paid me the great compliment of respect for my judgment and integrity, and entrusted to me what he said was "the greater portion" of his vast fortune, with the understanding that the legacy was to be presented to the American people.

This story has been written *to notify you of your right to share in this huge estate*, and to inform you of the conditions under which you may richly share it.

These conditions are in no way formidable or limited to the very few. The conditions are well within the reach of any adult of average intelligence. There are no tricks or false hopes, either in connection with the conditions or in this promise.

So that you may know whether or not this offers anything you need or desire, let me tell you specifically what is promised:

A clear description of the formula by which you may have the full benefit of the Master-Key to Riches—a key that should unlock the doors to the solution of all your problems, that will help you to convert your past failures into priceless assets, and lead you to attainment of the Twelve Great Riches, including economic security.

An inventory of the riches left by Andrew Carnegie for distribution to those who are qualified to receive them, together with detailed instructions through which you may acquire and use your full share.

A description of the means by which you may have the full benefit of the education, experience, and technical skills of those whose cooperation you may need for the attainment of your major purposes in life, thus providing a practical means by which you may bridge the disadvantages of an inadequate education and attain the highest goals of life as successfully as may those who are blessed with a formal education.

The privilege of using the philosophy of success which was organized from the life experiences, by trial and error, of hundreds of eminent men.

A definite plan by which anyone who works for wages or a salary may promote himself into a higher income *with the full cooperation and consent of his employer.*

A definite plan through which anyone who works for others may get into a business or profession of his own, with more than average chances of success.

A definite plan though which any businessman may convert his customers into permanent patrons, and through their hearty cooperation, add new customers who will likewise become permanent.

A definite plan by which any salesman of useful merchandise, or of services such as life insurance, may convert his buyers into willing workers who will aid him in finding new clients.

A definite plan through which any employer may make personal friends of his employees, under circumstances which will enable him to make his business more profitable for both himself and his employees.

You have here a clear statement of our promises, and the first condition under which you may benefit by these is that you read this book *twice*, line by line, and *think as you read*!

Let it be known at the outset that when we speak of "riches," we have in mind *all riches*—not merely those represented by bank balances and material things.

We have in mind the riches of liberty and freedom, of which we have more than any other nation. We have in mind the riches of human relationships through which every American citizen may exercise to the fullest the privilege of personal initiative in whatever direction he chooses. Thus, when we speak of "riches" we have reference to the abundant life which is everywhere available to the people of the United States, and obtainable with a minimum amount of effort.

Meanwhile, let it be understood that we shall offer no suggestions to anyone as to the nature of the riches for which he should aim, nor the amount he should undertake to acquire.

Fortunately, the American life offers an abundance of all forms of riches, sufficient in both quality and quantity to satisfy all reasonable human desires. We sincerely hope that every reader will aim for his share, not only of the things that money can buy, *but of the things money cannot buy*!

We shall not undertake to tell any man how to live his life, but we know, from having observed both the rich and poor of America, that material riches are no guarantee of happiness.

We have never yet found a truly happy person who was not engaged in some form of service by which others were benefited. And we do know many who are wealthy in material things, but have not found happiness.

We mention these observations not to preach, but to quicken those who, because of the great abundance of material riches in America, take them for granted, and who have lost sight of the priceless things of life that are to be acquired only through the intangible riches we have mentioned.

napoleonhill

Chapter One

THE TWELVE RICHES OF LIFE

You have, I believe, that human urge for the better things in life which is the common desire of all people. You desire economic security which money alone can provide. You may desire an outlet for your talents in order that you may have the joy of creating your own riches.

Some seek the easy way to riches, hoping to find it without giving anything in return. That too is a common desire. But it is a desire I shall hope to modify for your benefit, as from experience I have learned that there is no such thing as something for nothing.

There is but one sure way to riches, and that may be attained only by those who have the Master-Key to Riches. This Master-Key is a marvelous device which those who possess it may use to unlock doors to the solutions of their problems.

It opens the door to sound health.

It opens the door to love and romance.

It opens the door to friendship, by revealing the traits of personality and character which make enduring friends.

It reveals the method by which every adversity, every failure, every disappointment, every error of judgment, and every past defeat may be transmuted into riches of priceless value.

It kindles anew the dead hopes of all who possess it, and it reveals the formula by which one may "tune in" and draw upon the great reservoir of Infinite Intelligence.

It lifts humble men to positions of power, fame and fortune.

It turns back the hands of the clock and renews the spirit of youth for those who have grown old too soon.

It provides the method by which you may take full and complete possession of your own mind, thus giving you

1

unchallengeable control over the emotions of the heart and the power of thinking.

It bridges the deficiencies of those who have inadequate formal schooling, and puts them substantially on the same plane of opportunity that is enjoyed by those who have a better education.

And lastly, it opens the doors, one by one, to the Twelve Great Riches of Life which I shall presently describe.

No man may hear that for which he has not the preparation for hearing. The preparation consists of many things, among them sincerity of purpose, humility of heart, a full recognition of the truth that no man knows everything. I shall speak to you of facts and describe to you many principles, some of which you may never have heard, for they are known only to those who have prepared themselves to accept the Master-Key.

Your Two Selves

Before I describe the Twelve Great Riches, let me reveal to you some of the riches you already possess—riches of which you may not be conscious.

First, I would have you recognize that you are a plural personality, although you may regard yourself as a single personality. You and every other person consist of at least two distinct personalities, and many of you possess more.

There is that self which you recognize when you look into a mirror. That is your physical self. But it is only the house in which your other selves live. In that house there are at least two individuals who are eternally in conflict with each other.

One is a *negative* sort of person who thinks and moves and lives in an atmosphere of doubt and fear and poverty and ill health. This negative self expects failure and is seldom disappointed. It dwells on sorry circumstances of life which you want to reject but seem forced to accept—poverty, greed, superstition, fear, doubt, worry, and physical sickness.

Your "other self" is a *positive* sort of person who thinks in dynamic, affirmative terms of wealth, sound health, love and friendship, personal achievement, creative vision, service to others, and who guides you unerringly to the attainment of these blessings. It is this self alone which is capable

2

of recognizing and appropriating the Twelve Great Riches. It is the only self which is capable of receiving the Master-Key to Riches.

You have many other priceless assets of which you may not be aware, hidden riches you have neither recognized nor used. Among these is what we might call your "vibration center," a sort of radio broadcasting and receiving set of exquisite sensitivity, attuned to your fellow men and the universe around you. This powerful unit projects your thoughts and feelings and receives unending swarms of messages of great importance to your success in living. It is a tireless two-way communication system of infinite capacity.

Your radio station operates automatically and continuously, when you are asleep just as when you are awake. And it is under the control at all times of one or the other of your two major personalities—the negative personality or the positive personality.

When your negative personality is in control. your sensitive receivers register only the negative messages of countless negative personalities. Quite naturally, this leads to "what's the use?" and "I haven't got a chance" thinking; perhaps not formulated in just those words, but discouraging, if not deadly, to faith in yourself and the use of your energies to achieve what you desire. Negative messages received when your negative personality is in control of your receiving station, if accepted and used as a guide, invariably lead to circumstances of life that are the very opposite of what you would choose.

But when your positive personality is in control, it directs to your "action center" only those stimulating, high-energy optimistic, "I can do it" messages which you can translate into physical equivalents of prosperity, sound health, love, hope, faith, peace of mind and happiness—the values of life for which you and all other normal persons are searching.

The Greatest Gift

I wish to give you the Master-Key by which you may attain these and many other riches. Among other things, the Key places every individual radio station under the control of one's "other self," your positive personality.

3

I shall reveal to you the means by which you may share the blessings of the Master-Key, but the responsibility of sharing must become your own. Every close observer must have recognized that all individual successes which endure *have had their beginning through the beneficent influence of some other individual*, through some form of sharing.

I wish to share with you the knowledge by which you may acquire riches—*all riches*—through the expression of *your own personal initiative!*

That is the greatest of all gifts!

And it is the only kind of gift that anyone who is blessed with the advantages of a great nation like ours should expect. For here we have every form of potential riches available to mankind. We have them in great abundance.

I assume that you too wish to become rich.

I sought the path to riches the hard way before I learned that there is a short and dependable path I could have followed had I been guided as I hope to guide you.

First, let us be prepared to recognize riches when they come within our reach. Some believe that riches consist in money alone! But enduring riches, in the broader sense, consist of many other values than those of material things, and I may add that without these other intangible values the possession of money will not bring the happiness which some believe it will provide.

When I speak of "riches" I have in mind the greater riches whose possessors have made life pay off on their own terms—the terms of full and complete happiness. I call these the Twelve Riches of Life. And I sincerely wish to share them with all who are prepared to receive them.

1. A Positive Mental Attitude:

All riches, of whatever nature, begin as a state of mind; and let us remember that a state of mind is the one and only thing over which any person has complete, unchallenged right of control.

It is highly significant that the Creator provided man with control over nothing except the power to shape his own thoughts and the privilege of fitting them to any pattern of his choice.

4

Mental attitude is important because it converts the brain into the equivalent of an electro-magnet which attracts the counterpart of one's dominating thoughts, aims and purposes. It also attracts the counterpart of one's fears, worries and doubts.

A *positive mental attitude* (PMA) is the starting point of all riches, whether they be riches of a material nature or intangible riches.

It attracts the riches of true friendship, and the riches one finds in the hope of future achievement.

It provides the riches one may find in Nature's handiwork, as it exists in the moonlit nights, in the stars that float in the heavens, in the beautiful landscapes and in distant horizons.

And the riches to be found in the labor of one's choice, where expression may be given to the highest plane of man's soul.

And the riches of harmony in home relationships, where all members of the family work together in a spirit of friendly cooperation.

And the riches of sound physical health, which is the treasure of those who have learned to balance work with play, worship with love, and who have learned the wisdom of eating to live rather than of living to eat.

And the riches of freedom from fear.

And the riches of enthusiasm, both active and passive.

And the riches of song and laughter, both of which indicate states of mind.

And the riches of self-discipline, through which one may have the joy of knowing that the mind can and will serve any desired end if one will take possession and command it through definiteness of purpose.

And the riches of play, through which one may lay aside all of the burdens of life and become as a little child again.

And the riches of discovery of one's "other self"—that self which knows no such reality as permanent failure.

And the riches of faith in Infinite Intelligence, of which every individual mind is a minute projection.

And the riches of meditation, the connecting link by which anyone may draw upon the great universal supply of Infinite Intelligence at will.

Yes, these and all other riches begin with a positive mental attitude. Therefore, it is but little cause for wonder that a positive mental attitude takes the first place in the list of the Twelve Riches.

2. Sound Physical Health:

Sound health begins with a "health consciousness" produced by a mind which thinks in terms of health and not in terms of illness, plus temperance of habits in eating and properly balanced physical activities.

3. Harmony In Human Relationships:

Harmony with others begins with one's self, for it is true, as Shakespeare said, there are benefits available to those who comply with his admonition, "To thine own self be true, and it must follow, as the night the day, thou canst not then be false to any man."

4. Freedom From Fear:

No man who fears anything is a free man! Fear is a harbinger of evil, and wherever it appears one may find a cause which must be eliminated before he may become rich in the fuller sense.

The seven basic fears which appear most often in the minds of men are:

The fear of *poverty*.
The fear of *criticism*.
The fear of *ill health*.
The fear of *loss of love*.
The fear of the *loss of liberty*.
The fear of *old age*.
The fear of *death*.

5. The Hope of Achievement:

The greatest of all forms of happiness comes as the result of hope of achievement of some yet unattained desire. Poor be-

6

yond description is the person who cannot look to the future with hope that he will become the person he would like to be, or with the belief that he will attain the objective he has failed to reach in the past.

6. The Capacity For Faith:

Faith is the connecting link between the conscious mind of man and the great universal reservoir of Infinite Intelligence. It is the fertile soil of the garden of the human mind wherein may be produced all of the riches of life. It is the "eternal elixir" which gives creative power and action to the impulses of thought.

Faith is the basis of all so-called miracles, and of many mysteries which cannot be explained by logic or science.

Faith is the spiritual "chemical" which, when it is mixed with prayer, gives one direct and immediate condition with Infinite Intelligence.

Faith is the power which transmutes the ordinary energies of thought into their spiritual equivalent. And it is the only power through which the Cosmic Force of Infinite Intelligence may be appropriated to the uses of man.

7. Willingness to Share One's Blessings:

He who has not learned the blessed art of sharing has not learned the true path of happiness, for happiness comes only by sharing. And let it be forever remembered that all riches may be embellished and multiplied by the simple process of sharing them where they may serve others. And let it be also remembered that the space one occupies in the hearts of his fellowmen is determined precisely by the service he renders through some form of sharing his blessings.

Riches which are not shared, whether they be material riches or the intangibles, wither and die like the rose on a severed stem, for it is one of Nature's first laws that inaction and disuse lead to decay and death, and this law applies to the material possessions of men just as it applies to the living cells of every physical body.

7

8. A Labor Of Love:

There can be no richer man than he who has found a labor of love and who is busily engaged in performing it, for labor is the highest form of human expression of desire. Labor is the liaison between the demand and the supply of all human needs, the forerunner of all human progress, the medium by which the imagination of man is given the wings of action. And all labor of love is sanctified because it brings the joy of self-expression to him who performs it.

9. An Open Mind On All Subjects:

Tolerance, which is among the higher attributes of culture, is expressed only by the person who holds an open mind on all subjects at all times. And it is only the man with an open mind who becomes truly educated and who is thus prepared to avail himself of the greater riches of life.

10. Self-discipline:

The man who is not the master of himself may never become the master of anything. He who is the master of self may become the master of his own earthly destiny, the "master of his fate, the captain of his soul." And the highest form of self-discipline consists in the expression of humility of the heart when one has attained great riches or has been overtaken by that which is commonly called "success."

11. The Capacity To Understand People:

The man who is rich in the understanding of people always recognizes that all people are fundamentally alike, in that they have evolved from the same stem; that all human activities are inspired by one or more of the nine basic motives of life, viz:

The emotion of *love*
The emotion of *sex*
The desire for *material gain*
The desire for *self-preservation*
The desire for *freedom of body and mind*
The desire for *self-expression*
The desire for perpetuation of *life after death*
The emotion of *anger*
The emotion of *fear*

And the man who would understand others must first understand himself.

The capacity to understand others eliminates many of the common causes of friction among men. It is the foundation of all friendship. It is the basis of all harmony and cooperation among men. It is the fundamental of major importance in all leadership which calls for friendly cooperation. And some believe that it is an approach of major importance to the understanding of the Creator of all things.

12. Economic Security:

The last, though not least in importance, is the tangible portion of the "Twelve Riches."

Economic security is not attained by the possession of money alone. It is attained by the service one renders, for useful service may be converted into all forms of human needs, with or without the use of money.

A millionaire businessman has economic security, not because he controls a vast fortune of money, but for the better reason that he provides profitable employment of men and women, and through them, goods or services of great value to large numbers of people. The service he renders has attracted the money he controls, and it is in this manner that all enduring economic security must be attained.

Presently I shall acquaint you with the principles by which money and all other forms of riches may be obtained, but first you must be prepared to make application of these principles.

Your mind must be conditioned for the acceptance of riches just as the soil of the earth must be prepared for the planting of seeds.

When one is ready for a thing it is sure to appear!

This does not mean that the things one may need will appear without a cause, for there is a vast difference between one's *"needs"* and one's *readiness* to receive. To miss this distinction is to miss the major benefits which I shall endeavor to convey.

So be patient and let me lead you into *readiness* to receive the riches which you desire. I shall have to lead *my way*!

My way will seem strange to you at first, but you should not become discouraged on this account, for all new ideas seem strange. If you doubt that my way is practical, take courage from the fact that it has brought me riches in abundance.

Human progress always has been slow because people are reluctant to accept new ideas.

When Samuel Morse announced his system for communication by telegraph the world scoffed at him. His system was unorthodox. It was new, therefore it was subject to suspicion and doubt.

And the world scoffed at Marconi when he announced the perfection of an improvement over Morse's system; a system of communication by wireless.

Thomas A. Edison came in for ridicule when he announced his perfection of the incandescent electric light bulb, and the first auto-maker met with the same experience when he offered the world a self-propelled vehicle to take the place of the horse and buggy.

When Wilbur and Orville Wright announced the flight of a practical flying machine the world was so little impressed that newspaper men refused to witness a demonstration of the machine.

Then came the discovery of the modern radio, one of the "miracles" of human ingenuity which was destined to make the whole world akin. The "unprepared" minds accepted it as a toy to amuse children but nothing more.

I mention these facts as a reminder to you, who are seeking riches by a new way, that you be not discouraged because of the newness of the way. Follow through with me, appropriate my philosophy and be assured that it will work for you as it has worked for me.

By serving as your guide to riches I shall receive my compensation for my efforts in exact proportion to the benefits you receive. The eternal law of compensation insures this. My compensation may not come directly from you who appropriate my philosophy, but come it will in one form or another, for it is a part of the great Cosmic Plan that no useful service shall be rendered by anyone without a just compensation. "Do the thing," said Emerson, "and you shall have the power."

Aside from the consideration of what I shall receive for my endeavor to serve you, there is the question of an obligation which I owe the world in return for the blessings it has bestowed upon me. I did not acquire my riches without the aid of many others. I have observed that all who acquire enduring riches have ascended the ladder of opulence with two outstretched hands; one extended upward to receive the help of others who have reached the peak, and the other extended downward to aid those who are still climbing.

And here let me admonish you who are on the path to riches that you too must proceed with outstretched hands, to give and to receive aid, for it is a well known fact that no man may attain enduring success or acquire enduring riches without aiding others who are seeking these desirable ends. To *get* one must first *give!*

I have brought this message in order that I may *give!*

And now that we know what are the real riches of life I shall reveal to you the next step which you must take in the process of "conditioning" your mind to receive riches.

I have acknowledged that my riches came through the aid of others.

Some of these have been men well known to all who will hear my story. The men who have served as leaders in preparing the way for the rest of us, under that which we call *"The American way of life."*

Some have been strangers whose names you will not recognize.

Among these *strangers* are eight of my friends who have done most for me in preparing my mind for the acceptance of riches. I call them the Eight Princes. They serve me when I am awake and they serve me while I sleep.

Although I have never met the Princes face to face, as I have met the others who have aided me, they have stood watch over my riches; they have protected me against fear

11

and envy and greed and doubt and indecision and procrastination. They have inspired me to move on my own personal initiative, have kept my imagination active, and have given me definiteness of purpose and the faith to insure its fulfillment.

They have been the real "conditioners" of my mind, the builders of my *positive mental attitude!*

And now may I commend them to you so that they may render you a similar service?

Chapter Two

THE EIGHT PRINCES

You may call the Princes by another name if you choose. Mentors, perhaps. Or Principles. Or Counselors. Or Guardians of Good Spirit.

By whatever name, the Princes serve me through a technique that is simple and adaptable.

Every night, as the last order of the day's activities, the Princes and I have a round-table session. The major purpose is to permit me to express, and thus reinforce, my gratitude for the service they have rendered me during the day.

The conference proceeds precisely as if the Princes existed in the flesh. It is a time for meditation, review, and thanksgiving, with contact made through the power of thought.

Here you may receive your first test of your capacity to "condition" your mind for the acceptance of riches. When the shock comes, just remember what happened when Morse, and Marconi, and Edison, and the Wright Brothers first announced their perfection of new and better ways of rendering service. It will help you to stand up under the shock.

And now let us go into a session with the Princes:

GRATITUDE!

"Today has been beautiful.

"It has provided me with health of body and mind.

"It has given me food and clothing.

"It has brought me another day of opportunity to be of service to others.

"It has given me peace of mind and freedom from all fear.

"For these blessings I am grateful to you, my Princes of Guidance. I am grateful to all of you collectively for having unraveled the tangled skein of my past life, thereby freeing

13

my mind, my body and my soul from all causes and effects of both fear and strife.

"Prince of Material Prosperity, I am grateful to you for having kept my mind attuned to the consciousness of opulence and plenty, and free from the fear of poverty and want.

"Prince of Sound Physical Health, I am grateful to you for having attuned my mind to the consciousness of sound health, thereby providing the means by which every cell of my body and every physical organ is being adequately supplied with an inflow of cosmic energy sufficient unto its needs, and providing a direct contact with Infinite Intelligence which is sufficient for the distribution and application of this energy where it is required.

"Prince of Peace of Mind, I am grateful to you for having kept my mind free from all inhibitions and self-imposed limitations, thereby providing my body and my mind with complete rest.

"Prince of Hope, I am grateful to you for the fulfillment of today's desires, and for your promise of fulfillment of tomorrow's aims.

"Prince of Faith, I am grateful to you for the guidance which you have given me; for your having inspired me to do that which has been helpful to me, and for turning me back from doing that which had it been done would have proven harmful to me. You have given power to my thoughts, momentum to my deeds, and the wisdom which has enabled me to understand the laws of Nature, and the judgment to enable me to adapt myself to them in a spirit of harmony.

"Prince of Love, I am grateful to you for having inspired me to share my riches with all whom I have contacted this day; for having shown me that only that which I give away can I retain as my own. And I am grateful too for the consciousness of love with which you have endowed me, for it has made life sweet and all my relationships with others pleasant.

"Prince of Romance, I am grateful to you for having inspired me with the spirit of youth despite the passing of the years.

"Prince of Overall Wisdom, my eternal gratitude to you for having transmuted into an enduring asset of priceless value all of my past failures, defeats, errors of judgment and of deed, all fears, mistakes, disappointments and adversities of every nature; the asset consisting of my willingness and ability to

inspire others to take possession of their own minds and to use their mind-power for the attainment of the riches of life, thus providing me with the privilege of sharing all of my blessings with those who are ready to receive them, and thereby enriching and multiplying my own blessings by the scope of their benefit to others.

"My gratitude to you also for revealing to me the truth that no human experience need become a liability; that all experiences may be transmuted into useful service; that the power of thought is the only power over which I have complete control; that the power of thought may be translated into happiness at will; that there are no limitations to my power of thought save only those which I set up in my own mind."

My greatest asset consists in my good fortune in having recognized the existence of the Eight Princes, for it is they who conditioned my mind to receive the benefits of the Twelve Riches.

It is the habit of daily communication with the Princes which insures me the endurance of these riches, let the circumstances of life be whatever they may.

The Princes serve as the medium through which I keep my mind fixed upon *the things I desire* and off the things I do not desire!

They serve as a dependable fetish, a rosary of power, through which I may draw at will upon the powers of thought, with "each hour a pearl, each pearl a blessing."

They provide me with continuous immunity against all forms of negative mental attitude; thus they destroy both the seed of negative thought and the germination of that seed in the soil of my mind.

They help me to keep my mind fixed upon my major purpose in life, and to give the fullest expression to the attainment of that purpose.

They keep me at peace with myself, at peace with the world, and in harmony with my own conscience.

They aid me in closing the doors of my mind to all unpleasant thoughts of past failures and defeats. Nay, they aid me in converting all of my past liabilities into assets of priceless value.

The Princes have revealed to me the existence of that "other self" which thinks, moves, plans, desires and acts by the impetus of a power which recognizes no such reality as an impossibility.

And they have proved, times without number, that every adversity carries with it the seed of an equivalent benefit. So, when adversity overtakes me, as it overtakes everyone, I am not awed by it, but I begin immediately to search for that "seed of an equivalent benefit" and to germinate it into a full blown flower of opportunity.

The Princes have given me mastery over my most formidable adversary, myself. They have shown me what is good for my body and soul, and they have led me inevitably to the source and supply of all good.

They have taught me the truth that happiness consists not in the possession of things, but in the privilege of self-expression through the use of material things.

And they have taught me that it is more blessed to render useful service than to accept the service of others.

Observe that I ask for nothing from the Princes, but I devote the entire ceremony to an expression of gratitude for the riches they have already bestowed upon me.

The Princes know of my needs and supply them!

Yes, they supply all of my needs in over-abundance.

The Princes have taught me to think in terms of that which I can *give* and to forget about that which I desire to *get* in return. Thus they have taught me the proper approach to the *impersonal way of life:* that way of life which reveals to one the powers which come from within, and which may be drawn upon at will for the solution of all personal problems and for the attainment of all necessary material things.

They have taught me to be still and to listen from within!

They have given me the *faith* to enable me to override my reason and to accept guidance from within, with full confidence that the small still voice which speaks from within is superior to my own powers of reason.

My Creed of Life was inspired by the Princes.

Let me share it with you, so that you may adopt it as your Creed.

A Happy Man's Creed

I have found happiness by helping others to find it.

I have sound physical health because I live temperately in

16

all things, and eat only the foods which Nature requires for body maintenance.

I am free from fear in all of its forms.

I hate no man, envy no man, but love all mankind.

I am engaged in a labor of love with which I mix play generously. Therefore I never grow tired.

I give thanks daily, not for more riches, but for wisdom with which to recognize, embrace and properly use the great abundance of riches I now have at my command.

I speak no name save only to honor it.

I ask no favors of anyone except the privilege of sharing my riches with all who will receive them.

I am on good terms with my conscience. Therefore it guides me correctly in all that I do.

I have no enemies because I injure no man for any cause, but I benefit all with whom I come into contact by teaching them the way to enduring riches.

I have more material wealth than I need because I am free from greed and covet only the material things I can use while I live.

I own a great estate which is not taxable because it exists mainly in my own mind in intangible riches which cannot be assessed or appropriated except by those who adopt my way of life. I created this vast estate by observing Nature's laws and adapting my habits to conform therewith.

Workings of the Master-Key

Now let us get on with our story by a description of the philosophy one must adopt in order to acquire the Twelve Riches. I have described a method of preparing the mind to receive riches. But this is only the beginning of the story. I have yet to explain how one may take possession of riches and make the fullest use of them.

The story goes back more than half a century, and has its beginning in the life of Andrew Carnegie, a great philanthropist who was a typical product of the American system.

Mr. Carnegie acquired the Twelve Riches, the financial portion of which was so vast that he did not live long enough to enable him to give it away, so he passed much of it on

17

to men who are still engaged in using it for the benefit of mankind.

He was also blessed with the services of the Eight Princes. The Prince of Overall Wisdom served him so well that he was inspired not only to give away all his material riches, but to provide the people with a complete philosophy of life through which they too might acquire riches.

That philosophy consists of seventeen principles which conform in every respect to the pattern of the Constitution of the United States and the American system of free enterprise.

Mr. Carnegie explained his reason for having inspired the organization of a philosophy of individual achievement when he said:

"I acquired my money through the efforts of other people, and I shall give it back to the people as fast as I can find ways to do so *without inspiring the desire for something for nothing*. But the major portion of my riches consists in the knowledge with which I acquired both the tangible and the intangible portions of it. Therefore, it is my wish that this knowledge be organized into a philosophy and made available to every person who seeks an opportunity for self-determination under the American form of economics."

It is the philosophy which you must adopt and apply if you hope to accept the riches I desire to share with you.

Before I describe the principles of this philosophy I wish to give a brief history of what it has already accomplished for other men throughout more than half the world.

It has been translated into four of the leading Indian dialects and has been made available to more than 2,000,000 people of India.

It has been translated into the Portuguese language for the benefit of the people of Brazil, where it has served more than 1,500,000 people.

It has been published in a special edition for distribution throughout the great British Empire, where it has served more than 2,000,000 people.

It has benefitted one or more people in practically every city, town and village in the United States, numbering in all an estimated 20,000,000 people.

And it may well become the means of bringing about a better spirit of friendly cooperation between all the peoples of the world, since it is founded on no creed or brand, but consists of the fundamentals of all enduring success, and all constructive human achievements in every field of human endeavor.

It *supports all religions* yet it is a part of none!

It is so universal in its nature that it leads men inevitably to success in all occupations.

But more important to you than all of this evidence, the philosophy is so simple that you may start, right where you stand, to put it to work for you.

So, we come now to the description of the secrets of the Master-Key to all riches!

The seventeen principles will serve as a dependable road-map leading directly to the source of all riches, whether they be intangible or material riches. Follow the map and you cannot miss the way, but be prepared to comply with all of the instructions and to assume all of the responsibilities that go with the possession of great riches. And above all, remember that enduring riches must be shared with others; that there is a price one must pay for everything he acquires.

The Master-Key will not be revealed through any one of these seventeen principles, for its secret consists in the combination of all of them.

These principles represent seventeen doors through which one must pass to reach the inner chamber wherein is locked the source of all riches. The Master-Key will unlock the door to that chamber, and it will be in your hands when you have prepared yourself to accept it. Your preparation will consist of the assimilation and the application of the first five of these seventeen principles which I shall now describe at length.

19

Chapter Three

DEFINITENESS OF PURPOSE

It is impressive to recognize that all of the great leaders, in all walks of life and during all periods of history, have attained their leadership by the application of their abilities behind a *definite major purpose*.

It is not less impressive to observe that those who are classified as failures have no such purpose, but go around and around, like a ship without a rudder, coming back always empty-handed, to their starting point.

Some of these "failures" begin with a definite major purpose but they desert that purpose the moment they are overtaken by temporary defeat or strenuous opposition. They give up and quit, not knowing that there is a philosophy of success which is as dependable and as definite as the rules of mathematics, and never suspecting that temporary defeat is but a testing ground which may prove a blessing in disguise if it is not accepted as final.

It is one of the great tragedies of civilization that ninety-eight out of every one hundred persons go all the way through life without coming within sight of anything that even approximates definiteness of a major purpose!

Mr. Carnegie's first test, which he applied to all of his associate workers who were under consideration for promotion to supervisory positions, was that of determining to what extent they were willing to *go the extra mile*. His second test was to determine whether or not they had their minds fixed upon a definite goal, including the necessary preparation for the attainment of that goal.

"When I asked Mr. Carnegie for my first promotion," said Charles M. Schwab, "he grinned broadly and replied, *'if you have your heart fixed on what you want there is nothing I can do to stop you from getting it.'* "

20

Mr. Schwab knew what he wanted! It was the biggest job within Carnegie's control.

And Mr. Carnegie helped him to get it.

One of the strange facts concerning men who move with definiteness of purpose is the readiness with which the world steps aside that they may pass, even coming to their aid in carrying out their aims.

A Philosophy is Born

The story behind the organization of this philosophy is one with dramatic connotations in connection with the importance that Andrew Carnegie placed upon definiteness of purpose.

He had developed his great steel industry and accumulated a huge fortune in money when he turned his interest to the use and the disposition of his fortune. Having recognized that the better portion of his riches consisted in the knowledge with which he had accumulated material riches and in his understanding of human relationships, his major aim in life became that of inspiring someone to organize a philosophy that would convey this knowledge to all who might desire it.

He was then well along in years and he recognized that the job called for the services of a young man who had the time and the inclination to spend twenty years or more in research into the causes of individual achievement.

When I met Mr. Carnegie by mere chance (having come to interview him for the story of his achievements for a magazine) he had already interviewed more than two hundred and fifty men whom he suspected might have such ability. He was accustomed to probing into the characters of men with keen insight and must have wondered if I might have the qualities for which he had long been searching, for he set up an ingenious plan to make a test.

He began by relating the story of his achievements. Then he began to suggest that the world needed a practical philosophy of individual achievement which would permit the humblest worker to accumulate riches in whatever amount and form he might desire.

For three days and nights he elaborated upon his idea, describing how one might go about the organization of such a philosophy. When the story was finished Mr. Carnegie was

21

ready to apply his test, to determine whether or not he had found the man who could be depended upon to carry his idea through to completion.

"You now have my idea of a new philosophy," said he, "and I wish to ask you a question in connection with it which I want you to answer by a simple 'yes' or 'no'. The question is this:

"If I give you the opportunity to organize the world's first philosophy of individual achievement, and introduce you to men who can and will collaborate with you in the work of organization, do you wish the opportunity, and will you follow through with it to completion if it is given to you?"

I cleared my throat, stammered for a few seconds, then replied in a brief but fateful sentence.

"Yes," I exclaimed, "I will not only undertake the job, but I will finish it!"

That was definite! It was the one thing Mr. Carnegie was searching for—*definiteness of purpose*.

Many years later I learned that Mr. Carnegie had held a stop-watch in his hand when he asked that question, and had allowed exactly sixty seconds for an answer. If the answer had required more time the opportunity would have been withheld. The answer had actually required twenty-nine seconds.

And the reason for the timing was explained by Mr. Carnegie.

"It has been my experience," said he, "that a man who cannot reach a decision promptly, once he has all of the necessary facts for decision at hand, cannot be depended upon to carry through any decision he may make. I have also discovered that men who reach decisions promptly usually have the capacity to move with definiteness of purpose in other circumstances."

The first hurdle of the test had been covered with flying colors, but there was still another that followed.

"Very well," said Carnegie, "you have one of the two important qualities that will be needed by the man who organizes the philosophy I have described. Now I shall learn whether or not you have the second.

"If I give you the opportunity to organize the philosophy are you willing to devote twenty years of your time to research into the causes of success and failure, without pay, earning your own living as you go along?"

That question was a shock, for I had naturally suspected that I would be subsidized from Mr. Carnegie's huge fortune.

However, I recovered quickly from the shock by asking Mr. Carnegie why he was unwilling to provide the money for so important an assignment.

"It is not unwillingness to supply the money," Mr. Carnegie replied, "but it is my desire to know if you have in you a natural capacity for willingness to *go the extra mile* by rendering service before trying to collect pay for it."

Then he went on to explain that the more successful men in all walks of life were, and had always been, men who followed the habit of rendering more service than that for which they were paid. He also called attention to the fact that subsidies of money, whether they be made to individuals or to groups of individuals, often do more injury than good.

And he reminded me that I had been given an opportunity which had been withheld from more than two hundred and fifty other men, some of whom were much older and more experienced than I, and finished by saying:

"If you make the most of the opportunity I have offered you it is conceivable that you may develop it into riches so fabulous in nature as to dwarf my material wealth by comparison, for that opportunity provides the way for you to penetrate the keenest minds of this nation, to profit by the experiences of our greatest American leaders of industry, and it might well enable you to project your influence for good throughout the civilized world, thereby enriching those who are not yet born."

The opportunity was embraced!

I had received my first lesson on definiteness of purpose and a willingness to *go the extra mile*.

Twenty years later, almost to the day, the philosophy, which Mr. Carnegie had designated as being the better portion of his riches, was completed and presented to the world in an eight volume edition.

"And what of the man who spent twenty years of time without pay?" some ask. "What compensation has been received for this labor?"

A complete answer to this question would be impossible, for the man himself does not know the total value of the

23

benefits received. Moreover, some of these benefits are so flexible in nature that they will continue to aid him the remainder of his life.

But, for the satisfaction of those who measure riches in material values alone, it can be stated that one book, the result of the knowledge gained from the application of the principle of *going the extra mile*, has already yielded an estimated profit of upward of $3,000,000.00. *The actual time spent in writing the book was four months.*

Definiteness of purpose and the habit of *going the extra mile* constitute a force which staggers the imagination of even the most imaginative of people, although these are but two of the seventeen principles of individual achievement.

These two principles have been here associated for but one purpose. That is to indicate how the principles of this philosophy are blended together like the links of a chain, and how this combination of principles leads to the development of stupendous power which cannot be attained by the application singly of any one of them.

The Power of Definite Purpose

We come now to the analysis of the power of definiteness of purpose and psychological principles from which the power is derived.

First premise:
The starting point of all individual achievement is the adoption of a definite purpose and a definite plan for its attainment.

Second premise:
All achievement is the result of a motive or combination of motives, of which there are nine basic motives which govern all voluntary actions. (These motives have been previously described in Chapter One).

Third premise:
Any dominating idea, plan or purpose held in the mind, through repetition of thought, and emotionalized with a burning desire for its realization, is taken over by the subconscious

24

section of the mind and acted upon, and it is thus carried through to its logical climax by whatever natural means may be available.

Fourth premise:
Any dominating desire, plan or purpose held in the conscious mind and backed by absolute faith in its realization, is taken over and acted upon immediately by the subconscious section of the mind, *and there is no known record of this kind of a desire having ever been without fulfillment.*

Fifth premise:
The power of thought is the only thing over which any person has complete, unquestionable control—a fact so astounding that it connotes a close relationship between the mind of man and the Universal Mind of Infinite Intelligence, the connecting link between the two being *Faith.*

Sixth premise:
The subconscious portion of the mind is the doorway to Infinite Intelligence, and it responds to one's demands in exact proportion to the quality of one's *Faith!* The subconscious mind may be reached through faith and given instructions as though it were a person or a complete entity unto itself.

Seventh premise:
A definite purpose, backed by absolute faith, is a form of wisdom, and wisdom in action produces positive results.

The Major Advantages of Definiteness of Purpose

Definiteness of purpose develops self-reliance, personal initiative, imagination, enthusiasm, self-discipline and concentration of effort, and all of these are prerequisites for the attainment of material success.

It induces one to budget his time and to plan all his day-to-day endeavors so they lead toward the attainment of his *Major Purpose* in life.

It makes one more alert in the recognition of opportunities related to the object of one's *Major Purpose*, and it inspires

25

the necessary courage to act upon those opportunities when they appear.

It inspires the co-operation of other people.

It prepares the way for the full exercise of that state of mind known as *Faith, by making the mind positive* and freeing it from the limitations of fear and doubt and indecision.

It provides one with a *success consciousness*, without which no one may attain enduring success in any calling.

It overcomes the destructive habit of procrastination.

Lastly, it leads directly to the development and the continuous maintenance of the first of the Twelve Riches, a *positive mental attitude*.

These are the major characteristics of *Definiteness of Purpose*, although it has many other qualities and usages, and it is directly related to each of the Twelve Riches because they are attainable only by singleness of purpose.

Compare the principle of definiteness of purpose with the Twelve Riches, one at a time, and observe how essential it is for the attainment of each.

Then take inventory of the men of outstanding achievement which this country has produced, and observe how each of them has emphasized some major purpose as the object of his endeavors.

Thomas A. Edison devoted his efforts entirely to scientific inventions.

Andrew Carnegie specialized in the manufacture and sale of steel.

F. W. Woolworth centered his attention upon the operation of Five and Ten Cent Stores.

Philip D. Armour's specialty was that of meat packing and distribution.

James J. Hill concentrated on the building and maintenance of a great Transcontinental Railway System.

Alexander Graham Bell majored in scientific research in connection with the development of the modern telephone.

Marshall Field operated the world's greatest retail store.

Cyrus H. K. Curtis devoted his entire life to the development and publication of the *Saturday Evening Post*.

Jefferson, Washington, Lincoln, Patrick Henry and Thomas Paine devoted the better portion of their lives and their fortunes to a prolonged fight for the freedom of all people.

Men with singleness of purpose, each and every one!

And the list might be multiplied until it contained the name

26

of every great American leader who has contributed to the establishment of the American way of life as we of today know and benefit by it.

How to Acquire a Definite Major Purpose

The procedure in the development of a Definite Major Purpose is simple, but important, viz:

(a) Write out a complete, clear and definite statement of your *Major Purpose in Life*, sign it and commit it to memory. Then repeat it orally at least once every day, more often if practicable. Repeat it over and over, thus placing in back of your purpose all of your faith in Infinite Intelligence.

(b) Write out a clear, definite plan by which you intend to begin the attainment of the object of your *Definite Major Purpose*. In this plan state the maximum time allowed for the attainment of your purpose, and *describe precisely what you intend to give in return for the realization of your purpose*, remembering that there is no such reality as something for nothing, and that everything has a price which must be paid in advance in one form or another.

(c) Make your plan flexible enough to permit changes at any time you are inspired to do so. Remember that Infinite Intelligence, which operates in every atom of matter and in every living or inanimate thing, may present you with a plan far superior to any you can create. Therefore be ready at all times to recognize and adopt any superior plan that may be presented to your mind.

(d) Keep your *Major Purpose* and your plans for attaining it strictly to yourself except insofar as you will receive additional instructions for carrying out your plan, in the description of the *Master Mind Principle*, which follows.

Do not make the mistake of assuming that because you may not understand these instructions the principles here described are not sound. Follow the instructions to the letter; follow them in good faith, and remember that by so doing you are duplicating the procedure of many of the greatest leaders this nation has ever produced.

The instructions call for no effort that you may not easily put forth.

They make no demands upon time or ability with which the average person may not comply.

And they are completely in harmony with the philosophy of all true religions.

Decide *now* what you desire from life and what you have to give in return. Decide *where* you are going and *how* you are to get there. Then make a start from where you *now* stand. Make the start with whatever means of attaining your goal that may be at hand. And you will discover that to the extent you make use of these, other and better means will reveal themselves to you.

That has been the experience of all men whom the world has recognized as successes. Most of them started with humble beginnings with little more to aid them than a *passionate desire to attain a definite goal*.

There is enduring magic in such a desire!

And lastly, remember:

> "The Moving Finger writes; and, having writ,
>   Moves on: nor all thy Piety nor Wit
> Shall lure it back to cancel half a Line,
>   Nor all the Tears wash out a Word of it."

Yesterday has gone forever! Tomorrow will never arrive, but Today is yesterday's Tomorrow within your reach. What are you doing with it?

Presently I shall reveal to you a principle which is the keystone to the arch of all great achievements; the principle which has been responsible for our great American way of life; our system of free enterprise; our riches and our freedom. But first let us make sure that *you know what it is that you desire of life*.

Ideas that Lead to Success Begin as Definiteness of Purpose

It is a well known fact that ideas are the only assets which have no fixed values. It is equally well known that ideas are the beginning of all achievements.

Ideas form the foundation of all fortunes, the starting point

28

of all inventions. They have mastered the air above us and the waters of the oceans around us; they have enabled us to harness and use the invisible energies of the universe.

All ideas begin as the result of Definiteness of Purpose.

The phonograph was nothing but an abstract idea until Edison organized it through definiteness of purpose, and submitted it to the subconscious portion of his brain where it was projected into the great reservoir of Infinite Intelligence, from which a workable plan was flashed back to him. And this workable plan he translated into a machine which worked.

This philosophy of individual achievement began as an idea in the mind of Andrew Carnegie. He backed his idea with definiteness of purpose, and now the philosophy is available for the benefit of millions of people throughout the civilized world.

Moreover, his idea has more than an average chance of becoming one of the great leavening forces of the world, for it is now being used by an ever increasing multitude of people as a means of guiding them through a world of frenzied hysteria.

The great North American continent known as the "New World" was discovered and brought under the influence of civilization as the result of an idea which was born in the mind of an humble sailor and backed by definiteness of purpose. And the time is at hand when that idea, born more than four hundred years ago, may lift our nation to a position where it will become the most enlightened frontier of civilization.

Any idea that is held in the mind, emphasized, feared or reverenced, begins at once to clothe itself in the most convenient and appropriate physical form that is available.

That which men believe, talk about, and fear, whether it be good or bad, has a very definite way of making its appearance in one form or another. Let those who are struggling to free themselves from the limitations of poverty and misery not forget this great truth, for it applies to an individual just as it does to a nation of people.

Self-suggestion, the Connecting Link

Let us now turn our attention to the working principle through which thoughts, ideas, plans, hopes, and purposes

29

which are placed in the conscious mind find their way into the subconscious section of the mind, where they are picked up and carried out to their logical conclusion, through a law of nature which I shall describe later.

To recognize this principle and understand it is to recognize also the reason why Definiteness of Purpose is the beginning of all achievements.

Transfer of thought from the conscious to the subconscious section of the mind may be hastened by the simple process of "stepping up" or stimulating the vibrations of thought through faith, fear, or any other highly intensified emotion, such as enthusiasm, a burning desire based on definiteness of purpose.

Thoughts backed by faith have precedence over all others in the matter of definiteness and speed with which they are handed over to the subconscious section of the mind and are acted upon. The speed with which the power of faith works has given rise to the belief held by many that certain phenomena are the result of "miracles."

Psychologists and scientists recognize no such phenomenon as a miracle, claiming as they do that everything which happens is the result of a definite cause, albeit a cause which cannot be explained. Be that as it may, it is a known fact that the person who is capable of freeing his mind from all self-imposed limitations, through the mental attitude known as faith, generally finds the solution to all of his problems, regardless of their nature.

Psychologists recognize also that Infinite Intelligence, while it is not claimed to be an automatic solver of riddles, nevertheless carries out to a logical conclusion any clearly defined idea, aim, purpose or desire that is submitted to the subconscious section of the mind in a mental attitude of perfect faith.

However, Infinite Intelligence never attempts to modify, change or otherwise alter any thought that is submitted to it, and it has never been known to act upon a mere wish or indefinite idea, thought or purpose. Get this truth well grounded in your mind and you will find yourself in possession of sufficient power to solve your daily problems with much less effort than most people devote to worrying over their problems.

So-called "hunches" often are signals indicating that Infinite Intelligence is endeavoring to reach and influence the conscious section of the mind, but you will observe that they usually come in response to some idea, plan, purpose or desire, or some fear that has been handed over to the subconscious section of the mind.

All "hunches" should be treated civilly and examined carefully, as they often convey, either in whole or in part, information of the utmost value to the individual who receives them. These "hunches" often make their appearance many hours, days or weeks after the thought which inspires them has reached the reservoir of Infinite Intelligence. Meanwhile, the individual often has forgotten the original thought which inspired them.

This is a deep, profound subject about which even the wisest of men know very little. It becomes a self-revealing subject only upon meditation and thought.

Understand the principle of mind operation here described and you will have a dependable clue as to why meditation sometimes brings that which one desires, while at other times it brings that which one does not wish.

This type of mental attitude is attained only by preparation and self-discipline attained through a formula I shall describe later.

It is one of the most profound truths of the world that the affairs of men, whether they are circumstances of mass thought or of individual thought, shape themselves to fit the exact pattern of those thoughts.

Successful men become successful only because they acquire the habit of thinking in terms of success.

Definiteness of purpose can, and it should, so completely occupy the mind *that one has no time or space in the mind for thoughts of failure.*

Another profound truth consists in the fact that the individual who has been defeated and who recognizes himself as a failure may, by reversing the position of the "sails" of his mind, convert the winds of adversity into a power of equal volume which will carry him onward to success, just as,

> "One ship sails east, the other west,
>   Impelled by the self same blow,
> It's the set of the sails and not the gales,
>   That bids them where to go."

To some who pride themselves on being what the world calls "cool-headed, practical business men," this analysis of

31

the principle of Definiteness of Purpose may appear to be abstract or impractical.

There is a power greater than the power of conscious thought, and often it is not perceptible to the finite mind of man. Acceptance of this truth is essential for the successful culmination of any definite purpose based upon the desire for great achievements.

The great philosophers of all ages, from Plato and Socrates on down to Emerson and the moderns, and the great statesmen of our times, from George Washington down to Abraham Lincoln, are known to have turned to the "inner self" in times of great emergency.

We offer no apology for our belief that no great and enduring success has ever been achieved, or ever will be achieved, except by those who recognize and use the spiritual powers of the Infinite, as they may be sensed and drawn upon through their "inner selves."

Every circumstance of every man's life is the result of a definite cause, whether it is a circumstance that brings failure or one that brings success.

And most of the circumstances of every man's life are the result of causes over which he has or may have control.

This obvious truth gives importance of the first magnitude to the principle of Definiteness of Purpose. If the circumstances of a man's life are not what he desires, he may change them by changing his mental attitude and forming new and more desirable thought habits.

How Definiteness of Purpose Leads to Success

Of all the great American industrialists who have contributed to the development of our industrial system, none was more spectacular than the late Walter Chrysler.

His story should give hope to every young American who aspires to the attainment of fame or fortune, and it serves as evidence of the power one may gain by moving with Definiteness of Purpose.

Chrysler began as a mechanic in a railroad shop in Salt Lake City, Utah. From his savings he had accumulated a little more than $4,000, which he intended to use as a fund to set himself up in business.

32

Looking around diligently he decided that the automobile business was a coming industry, so he determined to go into that field.

His entry into the business was both dramatic and novel.

His first move was one that shocked his friends and astounded his relatives, for it consisted in his investing *all of his savings* in an automobile. When the car arrived in Salt Lake City he gave his friends still another shock by proceeding to take it apart, piece by piece, until the parts were scattered all over the shop.

Then he began to put the parts together again.

He repeated this operation so often that some of his friends thought he had lost his mind. That was because they did not understand his purpose. They saw what he was dong with the automobile, and it looked aimless and without purpose, but what they did not see was the plan which was taking form in Walter Chrysler's mind.

He was making his mind "automobile conscious!" Saturating it with Definiteness of Purpose! He was observing carefully every detail of the car. When he was through with his job of tearing down his automobile and rebuilding it, he knew all of its good points and all of its weak ones.

From that experience he began to design automobiles embodying all of the good points of the car he had bought and omitting all of its weaknesses. He did this job so thoroughly that when the Chrysler automobiles began to reach the market they became the sensation of the entire automobile industry.

His rise to fame and fortune was both rapid and definite, because he knew where he was going before he started, and he prepared himself with painstaking accuracy for the journey.

Observe these men who move with Definiteness of Purpose wherever you find them, and you will be impressed by the ease with which they attract the friendly co-operation of others, break down resistance and get that which they seek.

Analyze Walter Chrysler accurately and observe how definitely he acquired the Twelve Riches of life and made the most of them.

He began by developing the greatest of all the riches, a *positive mental attitude*.

That provided him with a fertile field in which to plant and germinate the seed of his Definite Major Purpose, the building of fine motor cars.

Then, one by one, he acquired other riches: sound physical health, harmony in human relationships, freedom from fear, hope of achievement, the capacity for faith, willingness to share his blessings, a labor of love, an open mind on all subjects, self-discipline, the capacity to understand people, and last, financial security.

One of the strangest facts concerning the success of Walter Chrysler consists in the simplicity with which he attained it. He had no appreciable amount of working capital with which to begin. His education was a limited one. He had no wealthy backers to set him up in business.

But he did have a practical idea and enough personal initiative to begin, right where he stood, to develop it. Everything he needed to translate his Definite Major Purpose into reality seemed almost miraculously placed in his hands as fast as he was ready for it—a circumstance which is not uncommon to men who move with definiteness of purpose.

A $2,000,000 Purpose

Shortly after *Think and Grow Rich* (a one-volume interpretation of a portion of the Andrew Carnegie philosophy of individual achievement) was published, the publisher began to receive telegraphic orders for the book from book stores in and near Des Moines, Iowa.

The orders called for immediate shipment of the book by express. The cause of the sudden demand for the book was a mystery until several weeks later, when the publisher received a letter from Edward P. Chase, a life insurance salesman representing the Sun Life Assurance Company, in which he said:

"I am writing to express my grateful appreciation of your book, *Think and Grow Rich*. I followed its advice to the letter. As a result I received an idea which resulted in the sale of a two million dollar life insurance policy. The largest single sale of its kind ever made in Des Moines."

The key sentence in Mr. Chase's letter is in the second sentence: "I followed its advice to the letter."

He moved on that idea with Definiteness of Purpose, and it helped him to earn more money in one hour than most life insurance men earn in five years of continuous effort.

34

In one brief sentence Mr. Chase told the entire story of a business transaction which lifted him out of the category of ordinary life insurance salesmen and made him a member of the coveted Million Dollar Round Table.

When he went out to sell a two million dollar life insurance policy he took with him a form of Definiteness of Purpose that was supported by faith. He did not merely read the book, as perhaps several million other men had done, and then lay it aside in an attitude of cynicism or doubt, with the thought that the principles it described might work for others but not for him.

He read it with an open mind, in a spirit of expectancy, recognized the power of the ideas it contained, appropriated those ideas, and moved on them with definiteness of purpose.

Somewhere in the book Mr. Chase's mind established contact with the mind of the author, and that contact quickened his own mind so definitely and intensely that an idea was born. The idea was to sell a life insurance policy larger than any he had ever thought of selling. The sale of that policy became his immediate Definite Major Purpose in life. He moved on that purpose without hesitation or delay, and behold! His objective was attained in less than an hour.

The man who is motivated by definiteness of purpose and moves on that purpose with the spiritual forces of his being, may challenge the man of indecision at the post and pass him at the grandstand. It makes no difference whether he is selling life insurance or digging ditches.

A definite, potent idea, when it is fresh in one's mind, may so change the biochemistry of that mind that it takes on the spiritual qualities which recognize no such reality as failure or defeat.

The major weakness of most men is that they recognize the obstacles they must surmount without recognizing the spiritual power at their command by which those obstacles may be removed at will.

The Road to Mastery

Riches—the real riches of life—increase in exact proportion to the scope and extent of the benefit they bring to those with whom they are shared. I know this to be true for I have grown rich by sharing. I have never benefitted anyone in any manner whatsoever without having received in return, from one source or another, ten times as much benefit as I have contributed to others.

One of the greatest of all truths which have been revealed to me is the fact that the surest way to solve one's personal problems is to find someone with a greater problem and help him to solve it, through some method of application of the habit of Going the Extra Mile.

This is a simple formula, but it has charm and magic, and it never fails to work.

However, you cannot appropriate the formula by the mere acceptance of my testimony as to its soundness. You must adopt it and apply it in your own way. You will then need no testimony as to its soundness.

You will find that many opportunities surround you.

By helping others to find the path *you will find it for yourselves!*

You might begin by organizing a Fellowship Club among your own neighbors or fellow workers, casting yourself for the role of leader and teacher of the group.

Here you will learn another great truth, namely, that the best way to appropriate the principles of the philosophy of individual achievement is by teaching it to others. When a man begins to teach anything he begins also to learn more about that which he is teaching.

You are now a student of this philosophy, but you can become a master of it by teaching it to others. Thus your compensation will be assured you in advance.

If you are a worker in industry here is your big opportunity to find yourself by helping others to adjust their relationships in peace and harmony. For soundness it has never been excelled, for it has been fully verified by the experiences of men in every walk of life.

Labor does not need agitators, but it does need *peacemakers.* It also needs a sound philosophy for the guidance of its following—a philosophy that benefits both the management and the workers. To this end the principles of this philosophy are perfectly suited.

The labor leader who guides his followers by this philosophy will have the *confidence of his followers and the fullest*

36

cooperation of their employers. Is that not obvious? Is it not sufficient promise of reward to justify the adoption of this philosophy?

A labor organization conducted by the principles of this philosophy would benefit everyone whom it affected. Friction would be supplanted by harmony in human relationships. Agitators and exploiters of labor would be automatically eliminated. The funds of the labor organization could be used for the education of its members and not for political intrigues.

And there would be more profits for distribution as wages— *profits which the management of industry would prefer to give to their workers instead of being forced to use them as a defense fund against the destructive efforts of agitators.*

There is a need for a Fellowship Club in every industry.

In the larger industries there is room for many such clubs.

The membership should consist of both the workers and the management, for here is a common meeting ground based upon principles on which everyone could agree. And agreement here would mean agreement at the workbench or the lathe.

I have emphasized this particular field of opportunity because I recognize that the chaos existing in the relationship between the management of industry and the workers constitutes *the number one economic problem of this nation.*

If you have not already adopted a Definite Major Purpose in life here is an opportunity for you to do so. You can start right where you are, by helping to teach this philosophy to those who are in need of it.

The time has come when it is not only beneficial to the individual to help his neighbor to solve his personal problems, *but it is imperative that each of us do so as a means of self-preservation.*

If your neighbor's house were on fire you would volunteer to help him put out the fire, even if you were not on friendly terms with him, for common sense would convince you that this would be the means of saving your own house.

In recommending harmony between the management of industry and the workers, I am not thinking of the interests of management alone, for I recognize that if this harmony does not prevail there soon will be *neither management nor workers as we know them today.*

On the other hand, the man with a sound philosophy of life

will find himself surrounded with an abundance of opportunities such as did not exist a decade ago.

The man who tries to get ahead without a Definite Major Purpose will meet with difficulties far greater than the average man can master.

The more lucrative opportunities of the world of today and tomorrow will go to those who prepare themselves for leadership in their chosen calling.

And leadership in any field of endeavor requires a foundation of sound philosophy. The days of the "hit and miss" leadership are gone forever. Skill and technique and human understanding will be required in the changed world we are now approaching.

The foremen and supervisors in industry must take on new responsibilities in the future. They must not only be skilled in the mechanics of their jobs, which is so essential for efficient production, but they must be skilled as well in the production of harmony among the workers for whom they are responsible.

The youngsters of today will become the leaders of our society tomorrow. What are we going to do about them? This is a problem of the first magnitude, and the major portion of the burden of solving it will fall upon the shoulders of the teachers in the public schools.

I mention these obvious facts as evidence that the future holds forth opportunities for useful service such as we have never known before; opportunities born of necessity in a world which has changed so rapidly that some fail to recognize the scope and the nature of the changes which have taken place.

Take inventory, you who are without a Definite Major Purpose, to find out where you fit in this changed world; prepare yourselves for your new opportunities and make the most of them.

Self-chosen Goals

If I had the privilege of so doing I could no doubt choose for you a Definite Major Purpose suited in every way to your qualifications and needs, and I might create for you a simple

38

plan by which you could attain the object of that purpose; but I can serve you more profitably by teaching you how to do this for yourself.

Somewhere along the way the idea for which you are searching will reveal itself to you. That has been the experience of most of the students of this philosophy. When the idea comes you will recognize it, for it should come with such force that you cannot escape it. You may be sure of that provided you are sincerely searching for it.

One of the imponderable features of this philosophy is that it inspires the creation of new ideas, reveals the presence of opportunities for self-advancement which had been previously overlooked, and inspires one to move on his own personal initiative in embracing and making the most of such opportunities.

This feature of the philosophy is not the result of chance. It was designed to produce a specific effect, since it is obvious that an opportunity which a man creates for himself, or an idea with which he may be inspired through his own thought, is more beneficial than any he may borrow from others, for the very procedure by which a man creates useful ideas leads him unerringly to the discovery of the source from which he may acquire additional ideas when he needs them.

While it is of great benefit to a man to have access to a source from which he may receive the inspiration necessary to create his own ideas, and self-reliance is an asset of priceless value, there may come a time when he will need to draw upon the resources of other minds. And that time is sure to come to those who aspire to leadership in the higher brackets of personal achievement.

Presently I shall reveal to you the means by which personal power may be attained, through the consolidation of many minds directed to the achievement of definite ends.

It was by this same means that Andrew Carnegie ushered in the great steel age and gave America its greatest industry, although he had no capital with which to begin, and very little education.

And it was by this means that Thomas A. Edison became the greatest inventor of all times, although he had no personal knowledge of physics, mathematics, chemistry, electronics or many other scientific subjects, all of which were essential in his work as an inventor.

It should give you hope to know that lack of education, lack of working capital, and lack of technical skill need not discourage you from establishing, as your major goal in life, any purpose you may choose, for this philosophy provides a way by which any goal within reason may be attained by any man of average ability.

The one thing it cannot do for you is to choose your goal for you!

But, once you have established your own goal, this philosophy can guide you unerringly to its attainment. That is a promise without qualifications.

We cannot tell you what to desire, or how much success to hope for, but we can and we shall reveal to you the formula by which successes may be attained.

Your major responsibility right now is to find out what you desire in life, where you are going, and what you will do when you get there. This is one responsibility which no one but you can assume, and it is a responsibility ninety-eight out of every hundred people never assume. *That is the major reason why only two out of every hundred people can be rated as successful.*

The Power of Burning Desire

Success begins through Definiteness of Purpose!

If this fact has seemed to be over-emphasized it is because of the common trait of procrastination which influences ninety-eight out of every hundred people to go all the way through life without choosing a Definite Major Purpose.

Singleness of purpose is a priceless asset—priceless because so few possess it.

Yet it is an asset which one may appropriate on a second's notice.

Make up your mind what you desire of life, decide to get just that, without substitutes, and lo! you will have taken possession of one of the most priceless of all assets available to human beings.

But your desire must be no mere wish or hope!

It must be a *burning desire*, and it must become so definitely an obsessional desire that you are willing to pay whatever price

40

its attainment may cost. The price may be much or it may be little, but you must condition your mind to pay it, regardless of what the cost may be.

The moment you choose your Definite Major Purpose in life you will observe a strange circumstance, consisting in the fact that ways and means of attaining that purpose will begin immediately to reveal themselves to you.

Opportunities you had not expected will be placed in your way.

The cooperation of others will become available to you, and friends will appear as if by a stroke of magic. Your fears and doubts will begin to disappear and self-reliance will take their place.

This may seem, to the uninitiated, a fantastic promise, but not so to the man who has done away with indecision and has chosen a definite goal in life. I speak not from the observation of other men alone, but from my own personal experience. I have transformed myself from a dismal failure to a successful man, and I have therefore earned the right to give you this assurance of what you may expect if you follow the road-map provided by this philosophy.

When you come to that inspiring moment when you choose your Definite Major Purpose, do not become discouraged if relatives or friends who are nearest you call you a "dreamer."

Just remember that the dreamers have been the forerunners of all human progress.

So, let no one discourage you from dreaming, but make sure you back your dreams with action based on Definiteness of Purpose. Your chances for success are as great as have been those of anyone who has preceded you. In many ways your chances are greater, for you now have access to the knowledge of the principles of individual achievement which millions of successful men of the past had to acquire the long and hard way.

He Knew What He Wanted

Lloyd Collier was born on a farm near Whiteville, North Carolina, in a family whose financial circumstances limited his chances of getting a formal education and forced him to begin at an early age to make his own way.

41

While he was still in his early teens he was stricken by a malady which paralyzed his body from his waist downward, a condition which would have justified him in sitting on a street corner with a tin cup and a pack of pencils.

Some business men in Whiteville raised a small fund and sent Lloyd to a school where he learned watch repairing. On his return he set up a work bench in the back of a small retail store, in rent-free space, and began to ply his trade as a watchmaker.

Despite his affliction, he never lost his self-confidence nor his cheerful disposition, two traits of personality that soon gained for him many friends and all the work he could do.

Lloyd came under the influence of the book *Think and Grow Rich*. It made such a profound impression upon him that he went to work in earnest to apply the famous Andrew Carnegie success formula described in the book.

His first step was that of writing out his *definite major aim*. He committed this to memory and repeated it many times daily. Substantially, it provided for him to own the finest jewelry store in Whiteville, marry the prettiest girl in the city, own the finest home and rear and educate a happy family of children.

Quite an order for a man without the use of his legs, starting from scratch and without operating capital.

But he made it! He attained every objective set down in his definite major aim. Moreover, he did it while he was still young enough to have a long road ahead of him for enjoying his well-earned blessings.

He gets around in a wheel chair and drives his own specially built car, getting in and out of it without help. His jewelry store is managed by trusted employees, with his wife in charge of the books. If you visited his store he would greet you enthusiastically from his wheel chair as you entered. And you would have the definite feeling that you were in the presence of a man whose physical affliction was by no means a handicap.

Lloyd Collier has adopted a habit which men with lesser physical afflictions than his might well copy. Each day he expresses a prayer of gratitude for the blessings he enjoys despite his physical handicap and each day he so lives and relates himself to his fellowmen that he does not seek pity. Instead, he seeks an opportunity to share some of his blessings with those who are more unfortunate than he, believing as he does that only by sharing them may he enrich and multiply his own blessings.

In Lloyd Collier we recognize the major difference between a man on a street corner, with a cup and a bunch of pencils, and a man who has made himself independent financially and has found peace of mind. The difference is mainly one of mental attitude. Lloyd discovered PMA (positive mental attitude) and through it found his way to everything he sought.

Any time you begin to feel sorry for yourself, or let NMA (negative mental attitude) get you down, take a trip to Whiteville, North Carolina, visit Lloyd Collier for a few hours, and you will come away with PMA written all over you.

Wise men share most of their riches generously. They share their confidences sparingly, and take great care not to misplace them. And when they talk of their aims and plans they generally do it by *action* rather than by words.

Wise men listen much and speak with caution, for they know that a man may always be in the way of learning something of value when he is listening, while he may learn nothing when he is speaking, unless it be the folly of *talking too much!*

There is always an appropriate time for one to speak and an appropriate time for one to remain silent. Wise men, when in doubt as to whether to speak or remain silent, give themselves the benefit of the doubt by keeping quiet.

Exchange of thought, through intercourse of speech, is one of the more important means by which men gather useful knowledge, create plans for the attainment of their Definite Major Purpose and find ways and means of carrying out these plans. And the "round table" discussions are an outstanding feature among men in the higher brackets of achievement. But these are far different from the idle discussions in which some men open their minds to anyone who wishes to enter.

Presently I shall reveal to you a safe method by which you may exchange thoughts with other men, with a reasonable assurance that you will *get* as much as you *give*, or more. By this method you may not only speak freely of your most cherished plans, but it will be profitable for you to so do.

I shall reveal to you an important intersection at which you may leave the by-path you are following on your way to success, and get on the main highway! The way will be clearly marked so that you shall not miss it.

This intersection of which I speak is the point at which men in the higher brackets of achievement come to a parting of the ways with many of their former associates and confidants, and join company with men who are prepared to give them a lift on their journey to riches.

Chapter Four

THE HABIT OF GOING THE EXTRA MILE

An important principle of success in all walks of life and in all occupations is a willingness to *Go the Extra Mile*; which means the rendering of more and better service than that for which one is paid, and giving it in a *positive mental attitude*.

Search wherever you will for a single sound argument against this principle, and you will not find it; nor will you find a single instance of enduring success which was not attained in part by its application.

The principle is not the creation of man. It is a part of Nature's handiwork, for it is obvious that every living creature below the intelligence of man is forced to apply the principle in order to survive.

Man may disregard the principle if he chooses, but he cannot do so and at the same time enjoy the fruits of enduring success.

Observe how Nature applies this principle in the production of food that grows from the soil, where the farmer is forced to *go the extra mile* by clearing the land, plowing it, and planting the seed at the right time of the year, for none of which he receives any pay in advance.

But, observe that if he does his work in harmony with Nature's laws, and performs the necessary amount of labor, Nature takes over the job where the farmer's labor ends, germinates the seed he plants and develops it into a crop of food.

And, observe thoughtfully this significant fact: For every grain of wheat or corn he plants in the soil, Nature yields him perhaps a hundred grains, thus enabling him to benefit by the law of *increasing returns*.

Nature *goes the extra mile* by producing enough of everything for her needs, together with a surplus for emergencies

45

and waste; for example, the fruit on the trees, the bloom from which the fruit is grown, frogs in the pond and fish in the seas.

Nature *goes the extra mile* by producing enough of every living thing to insure the perpetuation of the species, allowing for emergencies of every kind. If this were not true the species of all living things would soon vanish.

Some believe that the beasts of the jungle and the birds of the air live without labor, but thoughtful men know that this is not true. It is true that Nature provides the sources of supply of food for every living thing, but every creature must labor before it may partake of that food.

Thus we see that Nature discourages the habit which some men have acquired of trying to get something for nothing.

The advantages of the habit of *going the extra mile* are definite and understandable. Let us examine some of them and be convinced:

The habit brings the individual to the *favorable attention* of those who can and will provide opportunities for self-advancement.

It tends to make one indispensable, in many different human relationships, and it therefore enables him to command more than average compensation for personal services.

It leads to mental growth and to physical skill and perfection in many forms of endeavor, thereby adding to one's earning capacity.

It protects one against the loss of employment when employment is scarce, and places him in a position to command the choicest of jobs.

It enables one to profit by the law of contrast, since *the majority of people do not practice the habit.*

It leads to the development of a positive, pleasing mental attitude, which is essential for enduring success.

It tends to develop a keen, alert imagination because it is a habit which inspires one continuously to seek new and better ways of rendering service.

It develops the important quality of personal initiative.

It develops self-reliance and courage.

It serves to build the confidence of others in one's integrity.

It aids in the mastery of the destructive habit of procrastination.

It develops definiteness of purpose, insuring one against the common habit of aimlessness.

46

Give More, Get More

There is still another, and a greater reason for following the habit of *going the extra mile. It gives one the only logical reason for asking for increased compensation.*

If a man performs no more service than that for which he is being paid, then obviously he is receiving all the pay to which he is entitled.

He must render as much service as that for which he is being paid, in order to hold his job, or to maintain his source of income, regardless of how he earns it.

But he has the privilege always of rendering an overplus of service as a means of accumulating a reserve credit of goodwill, and to provide a just reason for demanding more pay, a better position, or both.

Every position based upon a salary or wages provides one with an opportunity to advance himself by the application of this principle, and it is important to note that the American system of free enterprise is operated on the basis of providing every worker in industry with a proper incentive to apply the principle.

Any practice or philosophy which deprives a man of the privilege of *going the extra mile* is unsound and doomed to failure, for it is obvious that this principle is the stepping-stone of major importance by which an individual may receive compensation for extraordinary skill, experience and education; and it is the one principle which provides the way of self-determination, regardless of what occupation, profession or calling the individual may be engaged in.

In America, anyone may earn a living without the habit of *going the extra mile*. And many do just that, but economic security and the luxuries available under the great American way of life are available only to the individual who makes this principle a part of his philosophy of life and lives by it as a matter of daily habit.

Every known rule of logic and common sense forces one to accept this as true. And even a cursory analysis of men in the higher brackets of success will prove that it is true.

The leaders of the American system are adamant in their demands that every worker be protected in his right to adopt and apply the principle of *going the extra mile*, for they recognize from their own experience that the future leadership in industry is dependent upon men who are willing to follow this principle.

It is a well known fact that Andrew Carnegie developed more successful leaders of industry than has any other great American industrialist. Most of them came up from the ranks of ordinary day laborers, and many of them accumulated personal fortunes of vast amounts, more than they could have acquired without the guidance of Mr. Carnegie.

The first test that Mr. Carnegie applied to any worker whom he desired to promote was that of determining to what extent the worker was willing to *go the extra mile*.

It was this test that led him to the discovery of Charles M. Schwab. When Mr. Schwab first came to Mr. Carnegie's attention he was working as a day laborer in one of the steel master's plants. Close observation revealed that Mr. Schwab always performed more and better service than that for which he was paid. Moreover, he performed it in a pleasing mental attitude which made him popular among his fellow workers.

He was promoted from one job to another until at long last he was made president of the great United States Steel Corporation, at a salary of $75,000 a year!

Not through all the ingenuity of man, or all the schemes that men resort to in order to get something for nothing, could Charles M. Schwab, the day laborer, have earned as much as $75,000 during his entire lifetime if he had not willingly adopted and followed the habit of *going the extra mile*.

On some occasions Mr. Carnegie not only paid Mr. Schwab's salary, which was generous enough, but he gave him as much as $1,000,000 as a bonus in addition to his regular salary.

When Mr. Carnegie was asked why he gave Mr. Schwab a bonus so much greater than his salary, he replied in words that every worker, regardless of his job or wages, might well ponder. "I gave him his salary for the work he actually performed," said Mr. Carnegie, "and the bonus for his willingness to *go the extra mile*, thus setting a fine example for his fellow workers."

Think of that! A salary of $75,000 a year, paid to a man who started as a day laborer, and a bonus of more than ten times that amount for a good disposition expressed by a willingness to do more than he was paid for.

The Habit of Going the Extra Mile ■

Verily it pays to *go the extra mile*, for every time an individual does so he places someone else under obligation to him.

No one is compelled to follow the habit of *going the extra mile*, and seldom is anyone ever requested to render more service than that for which he is paid. Therefore, if the habit is followed it must be adopted on one's own initiative.

But, the Constitution of the United States guarantees every man this privilege, and the American system provides rewards and bonuses for those who follow this habit, and makes it impossible for a man to adopt the habit without receiving appropriate compensation.

The compensation may come in many different forms. Increased pay is a certainty. Voluntary promotions are inevitable. Favorable working conditions and pleasant human relationships are sure. And these lead to economic security which a man may attain on his own merits.

There is still another benefit to be gained by the man who follows the habit of *going the extra mile: It keeps him on good terms with his own conscience and serves as a stimulant to his own soul!* Therefore it is a builder of sound character which has no equal in any other human habit.

You who have young boys and girls growing into adulthood might well remember this for their sake! Teach a child the benefits of rendering more service and better service than that which is customary, and you will have made contributions of character to that child which will serve him or her all through life.

The philosophy of Andrew Carnegie is essentially a philosophy of economics. But it is more than that! It is also a philosophy of ethics in human relationships. It leads to harmony and understanding and sympathy for the weak and the unfortunate. It teaches one how to become his brother's keeper, and at the same time rewards him for so doing.

The habit of *going the extra mile* is only one of the seventeen principles of the philosophy recommended to those who are seeking riches, but let us consider how directly it is related to each of the Twelve Riches.

First, this habit is inseparably related to the development of the most important of the Twelve Riches, a *Positive Mental Attitude.* When a man becomes the master of his own emotions, and learns the blessed art of self-expression through useful service to others, he has gone far toward the development of a positive mental attitude.

49

With a positive mental attitude as a builder of the proper thought-pattern, the remainder of the Twelve Riches fall into that pattern as naturally as night follows day, and as inevitably. Recognize this truth and you will understand why the habit of *going the extra mile* provides benefits far beyond the mere accumulation of material riches. You will understand also why this principle has been given first place in the philosophy of individual achievement.

Too Good a Man to Lose

Let us now observe that the admonition to render more service and better service than that for which one is paid, is paradoxical because *it is impossible for anyone to render such service without receiving appropriate compensation.* The compensation may come in many forms and from many different sources, some of them strange and unexpected sources, but come it will.

The worker who renders this type of service may not always receive appropriate compensation from the person to whom he renders the service, but this habit will attract to him many opportunities for self-advancement, among them new and more favorable sources of employment. Thus his pay will come to him indirectly.

Ralph Waldo Emerson had this truth in mind when he said (in his essay on Compensation), "If you serve an ungrateful master, serve him the more. Put God in your debt. Every stroke shall be repaid. The longer the payment is withholden, the better for you; *for compound interest on compound interest is the rate and usage of this exchequer.*"

Speaking once more in terms that seem paradoxical, be reminded that the most profitable time a man devotes to labor is that for which he receives no direct or immediate financial compensation. For it must be remembered that there are two forms of compensation available to the man who works for wages. One is the wages he receives in money. *The other is the skill he attains from his experiences;* a form of compensation which often exceeds monetary remuneration, for skill and experience are the worker's most important stock in trade through which he may promote himself to higher pay and greater responsibilities.

The Habit of Going the Extra Mile

The attitude of the man who follows the habit of *going the extra mile* is this: *He recognizes the truth that he is receiving pay* for schooling himself for a better position and greater pay!

This is an asset of which no worker can be cheated, no matter how selfish or greedy his immediate employer may be. It is the "compound interest on compound interest" which Emerson mentioned.

It was this very asset which enabled Charles M. Schwab to climb, step by step, from the lowly beginning as a day laborer to the highest position his employer had to offer; and it was this asset as well which brought Mr. Schwab a bonus of more than ten times the amount of his salary.

The million dollar bonus which Mr. Schwab received was his payoff for having put his best efforts into every job he performed—a circumstance, let us remember, which he controlled *entirely*. And it was a circumstance that could not have happened if he had not followed the habit of *going the extra mile*.

Mr. Carnegie had but little, if anything, to do with the circumstance. It was entirely out of his hands. Let us be generous by assuming that Mr. Carnegie paid off because he knew Mr. Schwab had earned the additional pay which had not been promised him. But the actual fact may be that he paid off rather than lose so valuable a man.

And here let us note that the man who follows the habit of *going the extra mile* thereby places the purchaser of his services under a double obligation to pay a just compensation; one being an obligation based upon his sense of fairness, the other based on *his sense of fear of losing a valuable man*.

Thus we see that no matter how we view the principle of *going the extra mile*, we come always to the same answer, that it pays "compound interest on compound interest" to all who follow the habit.

And we understand, too, what a great industrial leader had in mind when he said: *"Personally I am not so much interested in a forty hours per week minimum work law as I am in finding how I can crowd forty hours into a single day."*

The man who made that statement has an abundance of the Twelve Riches, and he freely admits that he attained his riches mainly by working his way up from a lowly beginning, applying the habit of *going the extra mile* every step of the way.

It was this same man who said, "If I were compelled to risk my chances of success upon but one of the seventeen

51

principles of achievement, I would, without hesitancy, stake everything on the principle of *going the extra mile*."

Fortunately, however, he was not obligated to make this choice, for the seventeen principles of individual achievement are related to each other like the links of a chain. Therefore they blend into a medium of great power through co-ordination of their use. The omission of any one of these principles would weaken that power, just as the removal of a single link would weaken the chain.

The power of the seventeen principles consists not in the principles, but in their *application and use!* When the principles are applied they change the "chemistry" of the mind from a negative to a positive mental attitude. It is this *positive mental attitude* which attracts success by leading one to the attainment of the Twelve Riches.

Each of these principles represents, through its use, a definite, positive quality of the mind, and every circumstance that draws upon the power of thought calls for the use of some combination of the principles.

The seventeen principles may be likened to the twenty-six letters of the alphabet through the combinations of which all human thought may be expressed. The individual letters of the alphabet convey little or no meaning, but when they are combined into words they may express any thought one can conceive.

The seventeen principles are the "alphabet" of individual achievement, through which all talents may be expressed in their highest and most beneficial form. Hence they provide the means by which one may attain the great Master-Key to Riches.

Chapter Five

LOVE, THE TRUE EMANCIPATOR OF MANKIND!

Love is man's greatest experience. It brings one into communication with Infinite Intelligence.

When it is blended with the emotions of sex and romance it may lead one to the higher mountain-peaks of individual achievement through *creative vision*.

The emotions of love, sex and romance are the three sides of the eternal triangle of achievement known as genius. Nature creates geniuses through no other media.

Love is an outward expression of the spiritual nature of man.

Sex is purely biological, but it supplies the springs of action in all creative effort, from the humblest creature that crawls to the most profound of all creations, man.

When love and sex are combined with the spirit of romance the world may well rejoice, for these are the potentials of the great leaders who are the profound thinkers of the world.

Love makes all mankind akin!

It clears out selfishness, greed, jealousy, and envy, and makes right royal kings of the humblest of men. True greatness will never be found where love does not abide.

The love of which I speak must not be confused with the emotions of sex, for love in its highest and purest expression is a combination of the eternal triangle, *yet it is greater than any one of its three component parts*.

The love to which I refer is the "elan vital"—the lifegiving factor—the spring of action—of all the creative endeavors which have lifted mankind to his present state of refinement and culture.

It is the one factor which draws a clear line of demarcation

53

between man and all of the creatures of the earth below him. It is the one factor which determines for every man the amount of space he shall occupy in the hearts of his fellowmen.

Love is the solid foundation upon which the first of the Twelve Riches may be builded, *a positive mental attitude*, and let us take heed that no man may ever become truly rich without it.

Love is the warp and the woof of all the remaining eleven riches. It embellishes all riches and gives them the quality of endurance, evidence of which may be revealed by cursory observation of all who have acquired material riches but have not acquired love.

The *habit* of *going the extra mile* leads to the attainment of that spirit of love, for there can be no greater expression of love than love which is demonstrated through service that is rendered unselfishly for the benefit of others.

Emerson had the vision of the kind of love to which I refer when he said: "*Those who are capable of humility, of justice, of love, of aspiration, are already on the platform that commands the sciences and arts, speech and poetry, action and grace.* For whoso dwells in this mortal beatitude does already anticipate those special powers which men prize so highly. . . .

"The magnanimous know very well that they who give time, or money, or shelter, to the stranger—so it be done for love, and not for ostentation—do, as it were, put God under obligation to them, so perfect are the compensations of the universe. In some way the time they seem to lose, is redeemed, and the pains they take, remunerate themselves. These men fan the flame of human love and raise the standard of civic virtue among mankind."

The great minds of every age have recognized love as the eternal elixir that binds the heart-wounds of mankind and makes men their brothers' keepers. One of the greatest minds this nation ever produced expressed his views on love in a classic that shall live as long as time endures. He said:

"Love is the only bow on life's dark cloud.

"It is the morning and the evening star.

"It shines upon the babe, and sheds its radiance on the quiet tomb.

"It is the mother of art, inspirer of poet, patriot and philosopher.

54

"It is the air and light of every heart—builder of every home, kindler of every fire on every hearth.

"It was the first to dream of immortality.

"It fills the world with melody—for music is the voice of love.

"Love is the magician, the enchanted, that changes worthless things to joy, and makes right royal kings and queens of common clay.

"It is the perfume of that wondrous flower, the heart, and without that sacred passion, that divine swoon, we are less than beasts; but with it, earth is heaven and we are gods.

"Love is transfiguration. It ennobles, purifies and glorifies. . . . Love is a revelation, a creation. From love the world borrows its beauty and the heavens their glory. Justice, self-denial, charity and pity are the children of love. . . . Without love all glory fades, the noble falls from life, art dies, music loses meaning and becomes mere motions of the air, and virtue ceases to exist."

If a man is truly great he will love all mankind!

He will love the good and the bad among all humanity. The good he will love with *pride* and *admiration* and *joy*. The bad he will love with *pity* and *sorrow*, for he will know, if he be truly great, that both good and bad qualities in men often are but the results of circumstances over which they have, because of their ignorance, little control.

If a man be truly great he will be compassionate, sympathetic and tolerant. When he is compelled to pass judgment upon others he will temper justice with tender mercy, throwing himself always on the side of the weak, the uninformed and the poverty-stricken.

Thus he will not only *go the extra mile* in a true spirit of Fellowship, but he will go *willingly and graciously*. And if the second mile be not enough he will go the third and the fourth, and as many additional miles as may be necessary.

Some Who Have Benefited by the Habit of Going the Extra Mile

No one ever does anything voluntarily without a motive. Let us see if we can reveal a sound motive that will justify the

55

habit of *going the extra mile* by observing a few who have been inspired by it.

Many years ago an elderly lady was strolling through a Pittsburgh Department Store, obviously killing time. She passed counter after counter without anyone paying any attention to her. All of the clerks had spotted her as an idle "looker" who had no intention of buying. They made it a point of looking in another direction when she stopped at their counters.

What *costly business* this neglect turned out to be!

Finally the lady came to a counter that was attended by a young clerk who bowed politely and asked if he might serve her.

"No," she replied, "I am just killing time, waiting for the rain to stop so I can go home."

"Very well, Madam," the young man smiled, "may I bring out a chair for you?" And he brought it without waiting for her answer. After the rain slacked the young man took the old lady by the arm, escorted her to the street and bade her good-bye. As she left she asked him for his card.

Several months later the owner of the store received a letter, asking that this young man be sent to Scotland to take an order for the furnishings of a home. The owner of the store wrote back that he was sorry, but the young man did not work in the house furnishings department. However, he explained that he would be glad to send an "experienced man" to do the job.

Back came a reply that no one would do except this particular young man. The letters were signed by Andrew Carnegie, and the "house" he wanted furnished was Skibo Castle in Scotland. The elderly lady was Mr. Carnegie's mother. The young man was sent to Scotland. He received an order for several hundred thousand dollars worth of household furnishings, and with it a partnership in the store. He later became the owner of a half interest in the store.

Verily it pays to *go the extra mile*.

Some years ago the editor of *The Golden Rule Magazine* was invited to deliver a speech at the Palmer School in Davenport, Iowa. He accepted the invitation on his regular fee basis, which was $100 and traveling expenses.

While the editor was at the college he picked up enough editorial material for several stories for his magazine. After he had delivered the speech and was ready to return to

Chicago he was told to turn in his expense account and receive his check.

He refused to accept any money for either his address or his expenses, explaining that he had already been paid adequately by the material he had procured for his magazine. He took the train back to Chicago feeling well repaid for his trip.

The following week he began to receive from Davenport many subscriptions to his magazine. By the end of the week he had received over $6,000.00 in cash subscriptions. Then followed a letter from Dr. Palmer explaining that the subscriptions had come from his students, who had been told of the editor's refusal to accept money which he had been promised and which he had earned.

During the following two years the students and the graduates of the Palmer School sent in more than $50,000 in subscriptions to *The Golden Rule Magazine*. The story was so impressive that it was written up in a magazine that had a circulation throughout the English-speaking world, and the subscriptions came from many different countries.

Thus, by rendering $100 worth of service without collecting, the editor had started the law of increasing returns to work in his behalf, and it yielded him a return of over 500 times his investment. The habit of *going the extra mile* is no pipe-dream. It pays, and pays handsomely!

Moreover, it never forgets! Like the other types of investments, the habit of *going the extra mile* often yields dividends throughout one's lifetime.

Let us look at what happened when one neglected an opportunity to *go the extra mile*. Late one rainy afternoon an automobile "salesman" sat at his desk in a New York show room which displayed expensive automobiles. The door opened and in walked a man jauntily swinging a cane.

The "salesman" looked up from the reading of the afternoon paper, took a swift glance at the newcomer, and immediately spotted him as another of those Broadway "window shoppers" who do nothing but waste one's valuable time. He went ahead with his newspaper, not taking the trouble to rise from his chair.

The man with the cane walked through the show room, looking first at one car and then another. Finally he walked over to where the "salesman" was sitting, teetered on his cane, and nonchalantly asked the price of three different automobiles on the floor. Without looking up from his newspaper, the "salesman" gave the prices and went on with his reading.

The man with the cane walked back over to the three automobiles at which he had been looking, kicked the tires of each one, then returned to the busy man at the desk and said, "Well, I hardly know whether I shall take this one, that one, the other one over there; or whether I shall buy all three."

The busy man at the desk responded with a sort of smirky, wiseacre smile, as much as to say, "Just as I thought!"

Then the man with the cane said, "Oh, I guess I will buy one of them. Send that one with the yellow wheels up to my house tomorrow. And, by the way, how much did you say it was?"

He took out his check book, wrote out a check, handed it to the "salesman," and walked out. When the "salesman" saw the name on the check, he turned fourteen different shades of pink and almost swooned from heart failure. The man who signed the check was Harry Payne Whitney, and the "salesman" knew that if he had only taken the time to get up from his chair he might have sold all three automobiles without any effort.

Withholding anything short of the best service of which one is capable is costly business—a fact which many have learned too late.

The right of personal initiative is not worth much to the fellow who is too indifferent or too lazy to exercise it. Many people are in this class without recognizing the reason they never accumulate riches.

Over forty years ago a young salesman in a hardware store observed that the store had a lot of odds and ends which were out of date and not selling. Having time on his hands, he rigged up a special table in the middle of the store. He loaded it with some of this unsalable merchandise, marking it at the bargain price of a dime an article. To his surprise and that of the owner of the store, the gadgets sold like hot cakes.

Out of that experience grew the great F. W. Woolworth Five and Ten Cent chain store system. The young man who stumbled upon the idea by *going the extra mile* was Frank W. Woolworth. That idea yielded him a fortune estimated at more than $50,000,000. Moreover, the same idea made several other persons rich, and applications of the idea are at the heart of many of the more profitable merchandising systems in America.

No one told young Woolworth to exercise his right to personal initiative. No one paid him for doing so; yet his action led to ever-increasing returns for his efforts. Once he put the idea into practice, increasing returns nearly ran him down.

There is something about this habit of doing more than one is paid for which works in one's behalf even while he sleeps. Once it begins to work, it piles up riches so fast that it seems like queer magic which, like Aladdin's Lamp, draws to one's aid an army of genii which come laden with bags of gold.

Some thirty years ago Charles M. Schwab's private railroad car was switched onto the siding at his steel plant in Pennsylvania. It was a cold, frosty morning. As he alighted from the car he was met by a young man with a stenographer's notebook in his hands who hurriedly explained that he was a stenographer in the general office of the steel company, and that he had come down to meet the car to see if Mr. Schwab needed any letters written, or any telegrams sent.

"Who asked you to meet me?" Mr. Schwab queried. "No one," the young man replied. "I saw the telegram coming through announcing your arrival, so I came down to meet you, hoping I might be of some service."

Think of that! He came down *hoping* he might be able to find something to do for which he was not paid. And he came on his own initiative without being told.

Mr. Schwab thanked him politely for his thoughtfulness, but said he had no need for a stenographer at the moment. After carefully noting the young man's name, he sent the lad back to his work.

That night, when the private car was hitched to the night train for its return to New York City it carried the young stenographer. He had been assigned, at Mr. Schwab's request, for service in New York as one of the steel magnate's assistants. The lad's name was Williams. He remained in Mr. Schwab's services for several years, during which opportunity after opportunity for promotion came to him unsolicited.

It is peculiar how opportunities have a way of trailing the people who make it their business to *go the extra mile*, but they do very definitely. Finally an opportunity came to young Williams which he could not ignore. He was made president and a large stockholder in one of the largest drug concerns in

59

the United States—a job which yielded him a fortune far greater than his needs.

This incident is clear evidence of what can happen, and of what has been happening all down through the years under the American way of life.

The habit of *going the extra mile* is one that does not confine its rewards to wage earners. It works as well for an employer as it does for an employee, as one merchant whom we knew quite well gratefully testified.

His name was Arthur Nash. His business was merchant tailoring. Some years ago Mr. Nash found his business just one step ahead of the sheriff. Conditions over which he seemed to have no control had brought him to the brink of financial ruin.

One of his most serious handicaps was that his employees had caught his spirit of defeatism and they expressed it in their work by slowing down and becoming disgruntled. His situation became desperate. Something had to be done, and it had to be done quickly if he were to continue in business.

Out of sheer desperation he called his employees together and told them the condition. While he was speaking, an idea occurred to him. He said he had been reading a story in *The Golden Rule Magazine* which told how its editor had *gone the extra mile* by rendering service for which he refused to accept pay, only to be voluntarily rewarded with more than $6,000 worth of subscriptions to his magazine.

He wound up by suggesting that if he and all of his employees caught that spirit and began to *go the extra mile* they might save the business.

He promised his employees that if they would join with him in an experiment he would endeavor to carry on the business, with the understanding that everyone would forget wages, forget working hours, pitch in and do his best, and take chances on receiving pay for work. If the business could be made to pay every employee would receive back wages with a bonus thrown in for good measure.

The employees liked the idea and agreed to give it a trial. The next day they began to come in with their meager savings, which they voluntarily loaned to Mr. Nash.

Everyone went to work with a new spirit, and the business began to show signs of new life. Very soon it was back on a paying basis. Then it began to prosper as it had never prospered before.

Ten years later the business had made Mr. Nash rich. The

employees were more prosperous than they had ever been, and everyone was happy.

Arthur Nash passed on, but today the business continues as one of the more successful merchant tailoring businesses of America.

The employees took over the business when Mr. Nash laid it down. Ask any one of them what he thinks of this business of *going the extra mile*, and you will get the answer!

Moreover, talk with one of the Nash salesmen, wherever you meet one, and observe his spirit of enthusiasm and his self-reliance. When this "extra mile" stimulant once gets into a man's mind, he becomes a different sort of person. The outlook on the world appears different to him, *and he appears different* because he is different.

Here is the appropriate place to remind you of an important thing about the habit of *going the extra mile* by doing more than one is paid for. *It is the strange influence which it has on the man who does it.* The greatest benefit from this habit does not come to those to whom the service is rendered. *It comes to the one who renders the service,* in the form of a changed "mental attitude," which gives him more influence with other people, more self-reliance, greater initiative, more enthusiasm, more vision and definiteness of purpose. All of these are qualities of successful achievement.

"Do the thing and you shall have the power," said Emerson. Ah, yes the *power!* What can a man do in our world without power? But it must be the type of power which attracts other people instead of repelling them. It must be a form of power which gains momentum from the *law of increasing returns*, through the operation of which one's acts and deeds come back to him greatly multiplied.

An Easy Way to Get What You Want

You who work for wages should learn more about this sowing and reaping business. Then you would understand why no man can go on forever sowing the seed of inadequate service and reaping a harvest of full grown pay. You would know that there must come a halt to the habit of demanding a full day's pay for a poor day's work.

And you who do not work for wages, but who wish to get

61

more of the better things of life! Let us have a word with you. Why do you not become wise and start getting what you wish the easy and sure way? Yes, there is an easy and a sure way to promote one's self into whatever he wants from life, and its secret becomes known to every person who makes it his business to *go the extra mile*. The secret can be uncovered in no other manner, *for it is wrapped up in that extra mile*.

The pot of gold at the "end of the rainbow" is not a mere fairy tale! The end of that *extra mile* is the spot where the rainbow ends, and that is where the pot of gold is hidden.

Few people ever catch up with the "end of the rainbow." When one gets to where he thought the rainbow ended he finds it is still far in the distance. The trouble with most of us is that we do not know how to follow rainbows. Those who know the secret know that the end of the rainbow can be reached only by *going the extra mile*.

Late one afternoon, some forty-five years ago, William C. Durant, the founder of General Motors, walked into his bank after banking hours, and asked for some favor which in the ordinary course of business should have been requested during banking hours.

The man who granted the favor was Carol Downes, an under official of the bank. He not only served Mr. Durant with efficiency, but he went the Extra Mile and *added courtesy to the service*. He made Mr. Durant feel that it was a real pleasure to serve him. The incident seemed trivial, and of itself it was of little importance. Unknown to Mr. Downes, this courtesy was destined to have repercussions of a far-reaching nature.

The next day Mr. Durant asked Downes to come to his office. That visit led to the offer of a position which Downes accepted. He was given a desk in a general office where nearly a hundred other people worked, and he was notified that the office hours were from 8:30 a.m. to 5:30 p.m. His salary to begin with was modest.

At the end of the first day, when the gong rang announcing the close of the day's work, Downes noticed that everyone grabbed his hat and coat and made a rush for the door. He sat still, waiting for the others to leave the office. After they had gone he remained at his desk, pondering in his own mind the cause of the great haste everyone had shown to get away on the very second of quitting time.

Fifteen minutes later Mr. Durant opened the door of his

private office, saw Downes still at his desk, and asked Downes whether he understood that he was privileged to stop work at 5:30.

"Oh yes," Downes replied, "but I did not wish to be run over in the rush." Then he asked if he could be of any service to Mr. Durant. He was told he might find a pencil for the motor magnate. He got the pencil, ran it through the pencil sharpener and took it to Mr. Durant. Mr. Durant thanked him and said "good night."

The next day at quitting time Downes remained at his desk again after the "rush" was over. This time he waited with purpose aforethought. In a little while Mr. Durant came out of his private office and asked again if Downes did not understand that 5:30 was the time for closing.

"Yes." Downes smiled. "I understand it is quitting time for the others, but I have heard no one say that I have to leave the office when the day is officially closed, so I chose to remain here with the hope that I might be of some slight service to you."

"What an unusual *hope*," Durant exclaimed. "Where did you get the idea?"

"I got it from the scene I witness here at closing time every day," Downes replied. Mr. Durant grunted some reply which Downes did not hear distinctly and returned to his office.

From then on Downes always remained at his desk after closing time until he saw Mr. Durant leave for the day. He was not paid to remain over time. No one told him to do it. No one promised him anything for remaining, and as far as the casual observer might know, *he was wasting his time.*

Several months later Downes was called into Mr. Durant's office and informed that he had been chosen to go out to a new plant that had been purchased recently to supervise the installation of the plant machinery. Imagine that! A former bank official becoming a machinery expert in a few months.

Without quibbling, Downes accepted the assignment and went on his way. He did not say, "Why, Mr. Durant, I know nothing about the installation of machinery." He did not say, "That's not my job," or "I'm not paid to install machinery." No, he went to work and did what was requested of him. Moreover, he went at the job with a pleasant "mental attitude."

Three months later the job was completed. It was done so well that Mr. Durant called Downes into his office and asked him where he learned about machinery. "Oh," Downes explained, "I never learned, Mr. Durant. I merely looked around, found men who knew how to get the job done, put them to work, and *they did it*."

"Splendid!" Mr. Durant exclaimed. "There are two types of men who are valuable. One is the fellow who can do something and do it well, without complaining that he is being overworked. The other is the fellow who can get other people to do things well, without complaining. You are both types wrapped into one package."

Downes thanked him for the compliment and turned to go.

"Wait a moment," Durant requested. "I forgot to tell you that you are the new manager of the plant you have installed, and your salary to start with is $50,000.00 a year."

The following ten years of association with Mr. Durant was worth between ten and twelve million dollars to Carol Downes. He became an intimate advisor of the motor king and made himself rich as a result.

The main trouble with so many of us is that we see men who have "arrived" and we weigh them in the hour of their triumph without taking the trouble to find out how or why they "arrived."

There is nothing very dramatic about the story of Carol Downes. The incidents mentioned occurred during the day's business, without even a passing notice by the average person who worked along with Downes. And we doubt not that many of these fellow-workers envied him because they believed he had been favored by Mr. Durant, through some sort of pull or luck, or whatever it is that men who do not succeed use as an excuse to explain their own lack of progress.

Well, to be candid, Downes did have an inside "pull" with Mr. Durant!

He created that "pull" on his own initiative.

He created it by *going the extra mile* in a matter as trivial as that of placing a neat point on a pencil when nothing was requested except a plain pencil.

He created it by remaining at his desk "with the hope" that he might be of service to his employer after the "rush" was over at 5:30 each evening.

He created it by using his right of personal initiative by finding men who understood how to install machinery instead of asking Durant where or how to find such men.

Trace down these incidents step by step and you will find

that Downes' success was due solely to his own initiative. Moreover, the story consists of a series of little tasks well performed, in the right "mental attitude."

Perhaps there were a hundred other men working for Mr. Durant who could have done as well as Downes, but the trouble with them was that they were searching for the "end of the rainbow" by running away from it in the 5:30 rush each afternoon.

Long years afterward a friend asked Carol Downes how he got his opportunity with Mr. Durant. "Oh," he modestly replied, "I just made it my business to get in his way, so he could see me. When he looked around, wanting some little service, he called on me because I was the only one in sight. *In time he got into the habit of calling on me.*"

There you have it! Mr. Durant "got into the habit" of calling on Downes. Moreover, he found that Downes could and would assume responsibilities by *going the extra mile*.

What a pity that all of the American people do not catch something of this spirit of assuming greater responsibilities. What a pity that more of us do not begin speaking more of our "privileges" under the American way of life, and less of the lack of opportunities in America.

Is there a man living in America today who would seriously claim that Carol Downes would have been better off if he had been forced, by law, to join the mad rush and quit his work at 5:30 in the afternoon? If he had done so, he would have received the standard wages for the sort of work he performed, but nothing more. Why should he have received more?

His destiny was in his own hands. It was wrapped up in this one lone privilege which should be the privilege of every American citizen: the right of personal initiative through the exercise of which he made it a habit always to *go the extra mile*. That tells the whole story. There is no other secret to Downes' success. He admits it, and everyone familiar with the circumstances of his promotion from poverty to riches knows it.

There is one thing no one seems to know: Why are there so few men who, like Carol Downs, discover the power implicit in doing more than one is paid for? It has in it the seed of all great achievement. It is the secret of all noteworthy success, and yet it is so little understood that most people look upon it as some clever trick with which employers try to get more work out of their employees.

Just after the end of the Spanish-American War, Elbert Hubbard wrote a story entitled *A Message to Garcia*. He told briefly how President William McKinley commissioned a young soldier by the name of Rowan to carry a message from the United States Government to Garcia, the rebel chieftain, whose exact whereabouts were not known.

The young soldier took the message, made his way through the fastnesses of the Cuban jungle, finally found Garcia, and delivered the note to him. That was all there was to the story—just a private soldier carrying out his orders under difficulties, and getting the job done without coming back with an excuse.

The story fired imaginations and spread all over the world. The simple act of a man doing what he was told, and doing it well, became news of the first magnitude. *A Message to Garcia* was printed in booklet form and the sales reached an all-time high for such publications, amounting to more than ten million copies. This one story made Elbert Hubbard famous, to say nothing of helping to make him rich.

The story was translated into several foreign languages. The Japanese Government had it printed and distributed to every Japanese soldier during the Japanese-Russian war. The Pennsylvania Railroad Company presented a copy of it to each of their thousands of employees. The big life insurance companies of America presented it to their salesmen. Long after Elbert Hubbard went down on the ill-fated Lusitania in 1915, *A Message To Garcia* continued as a best-seller throughout America.

The story was popular because it had in it something of the magic power that belongs to the man who does something, and does it well.

The whole world is clamoring for such men. They are needed and wanted in every walk of life. American industry has always had princely berths for men who can and will assume responsibilities and who get the job done in the right "mental attitude," by *going the extra mile*.

Andrew Carnegie lifted no fewer than forty such men from the lowly station of day laborers to millionaires. He understood the value of men who were willing to *go the extra mile*. Wherever he found such a man, he brought "his find" into the

66

inner circle of his business and gave him an opportunity to earn "all he was worth."

People do things or refrain from doing them because of a motive. The soundest of motives for the habit of *going the extra mile* is the fact that it yields enduring dividends, in ways too numerous to mention, to all who follow the habit.

No one has ever been known to achieve permanent success without doing more than he was paid for. The practice has its counterpart in the laws of nature. It has back of it an impressive array of evidence as to its soundness. It is based on common sense and justice.

The best of all methods of testing the soundness of this principle is that of putting it to work as a part of one's daily habits. Some truths we can learn only through our own experience.

Americans want greater individual shares of the vast resources of this country. That is a healthy desire. The wealth is here in abundance, but let us stop this foolish attempt to get it the wrong way. Let us get our wealth by giving something of value in return for it.

We know the rules by which success is attained. Let us appropriate these rules and use them intelligently, thereby acquiring the personal riches we demand, and adding to the wealth of the nation as well.

The Case of the Greedy Employer

Some will say, "I am already doing more than I am paid for, but my employer is so selfish and greedy he will not recognize the sort of service I am rendering." We all know there are greedy men who desire more service than that for which they are willing to pay.

Selfish employers are like pieces of clay in the hands of a potter. Through their greed they can be induced to reward the man who renders them more service than he is paid to render.

Greedy employers do not wish to lose the services of one who makes a habit of *going the extra mile*. They know the value of such employees. Here, then, is the crow-bar and the fulcrum with which employers can be pried loose from their greed.

Any clever man will know how to use this crow-bar, not by

67

withholding the quality or quantity of service he renders, *but by increasing it!*

The clever salesman of his personal services can manipulate a greedy purchaser of his services as easily as a smart woman can influence the man of her choice. The effective technique is similar to that used by clever women in managing men.

The clever man will make it his business to become indispensable to a greedy employer by doing more work and better work than any other employee. Greedy employers will "give their eye teeth" before parting with such a man. Thus the alleged greed of employers becomes a great asset to the man who follows the habit of *going the extra mile.*

We have seen this technique applied at least a hundred times as a means of manipulating greedy employers through the use of their own weakness. Not once have we seen it fail to work!

On some occasions the greedy employer failed to move as quickly as expected, but that proved to be his hard luck because his employee attracted the attention of a competitive employer who made a bid for the services of the employee and secured them.

There is no way to cheat the man who follows the habit of *going the extra mile.* If he does not get proper recognition from one source, it comes voluntarily from some other source—usually when it is least expected. It always comes if a man does more than he is paid for.

The man who *goes the extra mile* and does it in the right kind of "mental attitude" never spends time looking for a job. He does not have to, for the job is always looking for him. Depressions may come and go; business may be good or poor; the country may be at war or at peace; but the man who renders more service and better service than he is paid for *becomes indispensable to someone and thereby insures himself against unemployment.*

High wages and indispensability are twin-sisters. They always have been and always will be!

The man who is smart enough to make himself indispensable is smart enough to keep himself continuously employed, and at wages which not even the most greedy labor leader would ask.

Most men spend their lives searching for the "breaks," waiting for opportunities to overtake them, depending upon

68

"luck" to provide them with their needs, but never come within sight of their goal because they have no definite goal. Therefore they have no *motive* to inspire them to form the habit of *going the extra mile*. They never recognize:

"The Worldly Hope men set their Hearts upon
Turns Ashes—or it prospers; and anon,
Like Snow upon the Desert's dusty face
Lighting a little Hour or two—is gone."

Their haste becomes waste! For they go round and round, like goldfish in a bowl, coming back always to the place from whence they started; coming back empty-handed and disappointed.

Riches may be attained by appointment only; by the choice of a definite goal and a definite plan for attaining it; also by the selection of a definite starting point from which to take off.

But, let no one make the mistake of assuming that the habit of *going the extra mile* pays off only in terms of material riches. The habit definitely helps one to tap the source of spiritual riches, and to draw upon that source for every human need.

The Revealing Story of Edward Choate

Some men who are smart, and others who are wise, have discovered the way to riches by the deliberate application of the principle of *going the extra mile* for pecuniary gain.

However, those who are truly wise recognize that the greatest pay-off through this principle comes in terms of friendships which endure throughout life, in harmonious human relationships, in a labor of love, in the capacity to understand people, in a willingness to share one's blessings with others, all of which are among the Twelve Riches of life.

Edward Choate is one who has recognized this truth and has found the Master-Key to Riches. His home is in Los Angeles, California, and his business is that of selling life insurance.

At the outset of his career as a life insurance salesman he made a modest living from his efforts, but he broke no records in that field. Through an unfortunate business venture he lost all of his money and found himself at the bottom of the ladder, and was forced to make a new start.

I said "an unfortunate business venture," but perhaps I should have said "a fortunate business venture," for his loss influenced him to stop, look, listen, *think*, and to meditate concerning the fates of men which seem to lift some to high places of achievement but condemn others to temporary defeat or permanent failure.

Through his meditations he became a student of the philosophy of individual achievement. When Mr. Choate reached the lesson on *going the extra mile* he was awakened by a keen sense of understanding he had never before experienced, and he recognized that the loss of material riches may lead one to the source of greater riches, consisting of one's spiritual forces.

With this discovery Mr. Choate began to appropriate, one by one, the Twelve Riches of life, beginning at the head of the list by the development *of positive mental attitude*.

For the time being he ceased to think about the amount of life insurance he might sell, and began to look around for opportunities to be of service to others who were burdened with problems they could not solve.

His first opportunity came when he discovered a young man out in the deserts of California who had failed in a mining venture and was facing starvation. He took the young man into his home, fed him, encouraged him and kept him in his home until he found a good position for him.

In thus casting himself for the role of the good Samaritan, Mr. Choate had no thought of pecuniary gain, for it was obvious that a poverty-stricken, broken-spirited boy might never become a prospective purchaser of life insurance.

Then other opportunities to help the less fortunate began to reveal themselves so rapidly that it seemed as if Mr. Choate had made of himself a magnet which attracted only those with difficult problems to be solved.

But the appearance was deceiving, for he was only passing through a testing period by which he might demonstrate his sincerity of purpose in helping others. A period, let us not forget, which everyone who applies the principle of *going the extra mile* must experience in one way or another.

Then the scene shifted, and the affairs of Edward Choate began to take a turn he probably had not expected. His life insurance sales began to mount higher and higher, until at last they had reached an all-time high level. And miracle of miracles, one of the largest policies he had ever written up to that time was sold to the employer of the young man of the desert whom he had befriended. The sale was made without Mr. Choate's solicitation.

Other sales began to come his way in the same manner, until he was actually selling more insurance, without any strenuous effort, than he had ever sold previously by the hardest kind of labor.

Moreover, he had tapped a field of life insurance salesmanship in which the policies he sold were of large amounts. Men of great responsibilities and extensive financial affairs began to send for him to counsel them in connection with their life insurance problems.

His business grew until it brought him that goal which is so greatly coveted by all life insurance men—Life Membership in the Million Dollar Round Table. Such a distinction is attained only by those who sell a minimum of a million dollars a year in insurance for three consecutive years.

So, in seeking spiritual riches Edward Choate also found material riches; found them in greater abundance than he had ever anticipated. Six brief years after he had begun to cast himself for the role of the good Samaritan, Mr. Choate wrote more than two million dollars of life insurance during the first four months of the year.

The story of his achievements began to spread throughout the nation. It brought him invitations to speak before life insurance conventions, for other life insurance salesmen desired to know how he had managed to lift himself to so enviable a position in that profession.

He told them! And quite contrary to the usual practice among men who have attained success in the upper brackets of achievement, he revealed the humility of heart by which he is inspired, frankly admitting that his achievements were the result of the application of the philosophy of others.

The average man who is successful has a tendency to try to convey the impression that his success is due to his own smartness or wisdom, but very seldom does he frankly give credit to his benefactors.

What a pity there are not more Edward Choates in the world!

For it is obvious to all who think accurately that no man

71

ever attains a high degree of enduring success without the friendly co-operation of others; nor does any man ever attain enduring success without helping others.

Edward Choate is as rich in material values as he needs to be. He is far richer in spiritual values, for he has discovered, appropriated and made intelligent use of all of the Twelve Riches of Life, of which money is the last *and the least in importance*.

Chapter Six

THE MASTER MIND

Definition: *An alliance of two or more minds blended in a spirit of perfect harmony* and co-operating for the attainment of a definite purpose.

Note well the definition of this principle, for it carries a meaning which provides the key to the attainment of great personal power.

The Master Mind principle is the basis of all great achievements, the foundation stone of major importance in all human progress, whether it be individual progress or collective progress.

The key to its power may be found in the word "harmony!"

Without that element, collective effort may constitute co-operation, but it will lack the power which harmony provides through co-ordination of effort.

The tenets of major importance in connection with the Master Mind principle are these:

Premise 1:

The Master Mind principle is the medium through which one may procure the full benefit of the *experience, training, education, specialized knowledge* and *native ability* of others, just as completely as if their minds were one's own.

Premise 2:

An alliance of two or more minds, in a spirit of *perfect* harmony for the attainment of a definite purpose, stimulates each individual mind with a high degree of inspiration, and may become that state of mind known as Faith! (A slight idea of this stimulation and its power is experienced in the relationship of close friendship and in the relationship of love.)

Premise 3:

Every human brain is both a broadcasting station and a

73

receiving station for the expression of the vibrations of thought, and the stimulating effect of the Master Mind principle stimulates action of thought, through what is commonly known as telepathy, operating through the sixth sense.

In this manner many business and professional alliances are translated into reality, and seldom has anyone ever attained a high station or enduring power without the application of the Master Mind principle through which he secured the benefit of other minds.

This fact alone is sufficient evidence of the soundness and the importance of the Master Mind principle, and it is a fact which anyone may observe without straining his powers of observation or over-taxing his credulity.

Premise 4:

The Master Mind principle, when actively applied, has the effect of connecting one with the subconscious section of the mind, and the subconscious sections of the minds of his allies—a fact which may explain many of the seemingly miraculous results obtained through the Master Mind.

Premise 5:

The more important human relationships in connection with which one may apply beneficially the Master Mind principle are these:

(a) In marriage
(b) In religion
(c) In connection with one's occupation, profession or calling.

The Master Mind principle made it possible for Thomas A. Edison to become a great inventor despite his lack of education and his lack of knowledge of the sciences with which he had to work—a circumstance which offers hope to all who erroneously believe themselves to be seriously handicapped by the lack of a formal education.

With the aid of the Master Mind principle one may understand the history and the structure of this earth on which we live through the knowledge of skilled geologists.

Through the knowledge and experience of the chemist one may make practical use of chemistry without being a trained chemist.

With the aid of scientists, technicians, physicists and practical mechanics one may become a successful inventor without personal training in any of these fields.

There are two general types of Master Mind alliances, viz:

1. Alliance, for purely social or personal reasons, with one's relatives, religious advisors and friends, where no material gain or objective is sought. *The most important of this type of alliance is that of man and wife.*

2. Alliances for business, professional and economic advancement, consisting of individuals who have a personal motive in connection with the object of the alliance.

Now let us consider some of the more important examples of power that have been attained by the application of the Master Mind.

The American form of government, as it was originally written into the Constitution of the United States, should have first analysis because it is one form of power which vitally affects every citizen of our country, and to a large degree affects the entire world.

Our country is noted for three obvious facts:

1. It is the richest country of the world.
2. It is the most powerful nation of the world.
3. It provides its citizens with more personal freedom than does any other nation.

Riches, freedom and power! What an awe-inspiring combination of realities!

The source of these benefits is not difficult to determine, for it centers in the Constitution of our country and in the American system of free enterprise, these having been so harmoniously coordinated that they have provided the people with both spiritual and economic power, such as the world has never before witnessed.

Our form of government is a stupendous Master Mind alliance made up of the harmonious relationship of all the people of the nation, functioning through fifty separate groups known as states.

The central core of our American Master Mind is easily discernible by breaking down our form of government and examining its component parts, all of which are under the direct control of a majority of the people.

These parts are:

1. The executive branch of our government (maintained by a President)
2. The judiciary branch (maintained by the Supreme Court)
3. The legislative branch (maintained by the two Houses of Congress)

75

Our Constitution has been so wisely constructed that the power behind all three of these branches of government is held by the people. It is a power of which the people cannot be deprived *except by their own neglect to use it!*

Our political power is expressed through our government.

Our economic power is maintained and expressed through our system of free enterprise.

And the sum total of the power of these two is always in exact ratio to the degree of harmony with which the two are coordinated!

The power thus attained *is the property of all the people!*

It is this power which has provided the people with the highest standard of living that civilization has yet evolved, and which has made our nation truly the richest and the freest and the most powerful nation of the world.

We speak of this power as "The American Way Of Life!"

It was this way of life and our desire to maintain it which brought about the consolidation of our forces, both economic and spiritual, in a war that threatened the destruction of civilization as well as our way of life.

The future of mankind may have been determined by the application of our American Master Mind, for it is obvious that ours was the balance of power which turned the tide of war in favor of freedom for all mankind.

Another illustration of the Master Mind applied to industry may be found in the great American systems of transportation and communications. The men who manage our railroads and our air lines, our telephone and telegraph systems, have established a service which has never been equaled in any other country. Their efficiency and the resultant power consist entirely in their application of the Master Mind principle of harmonious co-ordination of effort.

Still another example of power attained through the Master Mind principle may be found by observing the relationship of our military forces—our Armies, our Navy and our Air Forces. Here, as elsewhere, the keystone to the arch of our power has been *harmonious co-ordination of effort.*

The modern football team is an excellent example of power attained through harmony of effort.

The great American system of chain store merchandising is still another example of economic power attained through the Master Mind principle.

And every successful industry is the result of application of the Master Mind. The American system of free enterprise in its entirety is a marvelous illustration of economic power produced by friendly harmonious co-ordination of effort.

The Master Mind principle is not the exclusive property of the rich and the powerful, but it is the means of major importance by which men may attain desirable ends.

The humblest person may benefit from this principle by forming a harmonious alliance with anyone of his choice. The most profound, and perhaps the most beneficial application of this principle that any man may make is the Master Mind alliance in marriage, provided the motive behind that alliance is Love!

This sort of alliance not only co-ordinates the minds of man and wife, but it also blends the spiritual qualities of their souls.

The benefits of such an alliance not only bring joy and happiness to man and wife, but they profoundly bless their children with sound character, and endow them with the fundamentals of a successful life.

You now have an understandable interpretation of the greatest source of personal power known to men—the Master Mind. The responsibility for its right use is yours.

Use it well and you will be blessed with the privilege of occupying great space in the world; space that can be estimated in both geography and in human relationships which are friendly and cooperative.

Do not be afraid to aim high when you establish your goal.

Remember that you live in a land of opportunities where no man is limited in the quality, the quantity or the nature of the riches he may acquire, provided he is willing to give adequate value in return.

Before you fix your goal in life, memorize the following lines and take to heart the lesson they teach:

> "I bargained with Life for a penny,
>   And Life would pay no more,
> However I begged at evening
>   When I counted my scanty store.
>
> "For Life is a just employer,
>   He gives you what you ask,
> But once you have set the wages,
>   Why, you must bear the task.

"I worked for a menial's hire,
    Only to learn, dismayed,
That any wage I had asked of Life,
    Life would have *willingly paid*."

Successful men do not bargain with Life for poverty!

They know that there is a power through which Life may be made to pay off on their own terms. They know that this power is available to every man who comes into possession of the Master-Key to Riches. They know the nature of this power and its unlimited scope. They know it by a name of one word; the greatest word in the English language!

This word is known to all men, but the secrets of its power are understood by few.

Chapter Seven

ANALYSIS OF THE MASTER MIND PRINCIPLE

When I was commissioned by Andrew Carnegie to organize the philosophy of individual achievement I asked him to describe the Master Mind principle so it might be appropriated and used by others, for the attainment of their Definite Major Purpose.

"Mr. Carnegie," I requested, "will you define the Master Mind principle as it may be applied through the individual efforts of men and women who are seeking their places in the great American way of life? Describe, if you will, the various forms of application that may be made of this principle by the man of average ability, in his daily efforts to make the most of his opportunities in this country."

And this is Mr. Carnegie's reply:

"The privileges which are available to the American people have back of them a source of great power. But privileges do not spring, mushroom-like, from nothing. They must be created and maintained by the application of power.

"The founders of our American form of government, through their foresight and wisdom, laid the foundation for all of our American form of liberty, freedom and riches. But, they only laid the foundation. The responsibility of embracing and using this foundation must be assumed by every person who claims any portion of this freedom and wealth.

"I will describe some of the individual uses of the Master Mind principle, as it may be applied in the development of various human relationships which may contribute to the attainment of one's Definite Major Purpose.

"But first I wish to emphasize the fact that the attainment of one's Definite Major Purpose can be carried out only by a series of steps; that every thought one thinks, every

79

transaction in which one engages, in relationship with others, every plan one creates, every mistake one makes, has a vital bearing on his ability to attain his chosen goal.

"The mere choice of a Definite Major Purpose, even though it be written out in clear language and fully fixed in one's mind, will not insure the successful realization of that purpose.

"One's major purpose must be backed up and followed through by continuous effort, *the most important part of which consists in the sort of relationship one maintains with others*.

"With this truth well established in one's mind it will not be difficult for one to understand how necessary it is to be careful in one's choice of associates, especially those with whom one maintains close personal contact in connection with his occupation.

"Here, then, are some of the sources of human relationship, which the man with a Definite Major Purpose must cultivate, organize and use in his progress toward the attainment of his chosen goal:

Occupation

"Outside of the relationship of marriage (which is the most important of all Master Mind relationships) there is no form of relationship as important as that which exists between a man and those with whom he works in his chosen occupation.

"Every man has a tendency to take on the mannerisms, beliefs, mental attitude, political and economic viewpoint, as well as other traits of the more outspoken of the men with whom he associates in his daily work.

"The major tragedy of this tendency lies in the fact that not always is the most outspoken among one's daily associates the soundest thinker; and very often he is a man with a grievance, who takes pleasure in airing the grievance among his fellow workers.

"Also, the most outspoken man often is an individual who has no Definite Major Purpose of his own. Therefore he devotes much of his time endeavoring to belittle the man who has such a purpose.

"Men of sound character, who know exactly what they

80

wish, usually have the wisdom to keep their own counsel, and seldom waste any of their time trying to discourage others. They are so busily engaged in promoting their own purpose that they have no time to waste with anyone or anything which does not contribute in one way or another to their benefit.

"Realizing that one may find in almost every group of associates some person whose influence and cooperation may be helpful, the man of keen discrimination, who has a Definite Major Purpose he desires to attain, will prove his wisdom by forming friendships with those who can be, and who are willing to become, mutually beneficial to him. The others he will tactfully avoid.

"Naturally he will seek his closest alliances with men whom he recognizes possess traits of character, knowledge and personality which may become helpful to him; and of course he will not overlook those holding positions of higher rank than his own, keeping his eye on the day when he may not only equal such men, but excel them, remembering meanwhile the words of Abraham Lincoln, who said: 'I will study and prepare myself, and some day my chance will come.'

"The man with a constructive Definite Major Purpose will never envy his superiors, but he will study their methods and learn to acquire their knowledge. You may accept it as a sound prophecy that the man who spends his time finding fault with his superiors will never become a successful leader on his own account.

"The greatest soldiers are those who can take, and carry out, orders of their superiors in rank. Those who cannot or will not do this, never will become successful leaders in military operations. The same rule is true of any man in other walks of life. If he fails to emulate the man above him, in a spirit of harmony, he will never benefit greatly from his association with that man.

"No fewer than a hundred men have risen from the ranks in my own organization, and have found themselves richer than they need be. They were not promoted because of bad dispositions or the habit of finding fault with those above or those below them, but they promoted themselves by appropriating and making practical use of the experience of everyone with whom they came in contact.

"The man with a Definite Major Purpose will take careful

81

inventory of every person with whom he comes in contact in his daily work, and he will look upon every such person as a possible source of useful knowledge or influence which he may borrow and use in his own promotion.

"If a man looks about him intelligently he will discover that his place of daily labor is literally a school room in which he may acquire the greatest of all educations—that which comes from observation and experience.

"How may one make the most of this sort of schooling? some will ask.

"The answer may be found by studying the nine basic motives which move men to voluntary action. Men lend their experience, their knowledge, and they cooperate with other men, because they have been given a sufficient motive to cause them to desire as much. The man who relates himself to his daily associates in a friendly, cooperative way, with the right sort of mental attitude toward them, stands a better chance of learning from them than does the man who is belligerent, irritable, discourteous or neglectful of the little amenities of courtesy which exist between all cultured people.

"The old saying that 'a man can catch more flies with honey than with salt' might well be remembered by the man who wishes to learn of his daily associates who know more about many things than he does, and whose cooperation he needs and seeks.

Education

"No man's education is ever finished.

"The man whose Definite Major Purpose is of noteworthy proportions must remain always a student, and he must learn from every possible source, especially those sources from which he may acquire specialized knowledge and experience related to his major purpose.

"The public libraries are free. They offer a great array of organized knowledge on every subject. They carry, in every language, the total of man's knowledge on every subject. The successful man with a Definite Major Purpose makes it his business and his responsibility to read books relating to that purpose, and thus acquire important knowledge which comes from the experiences of other men who have gone before him. It has been said that a man cannot consider himself even a kindergarten student of any subject until he has availed himself, as far as reasonably possible, of all the knowledge on that subject which has been preserved for him through the experience of others.

"A man's reading program should be as carefully planned as his daily diet, for that too is food, without which he cannot grow mentally.

"The man who spends all of his spare time reading the funny papers and the sex magazines is not headed toward any great achievement.

"The same may be said of the man who does not include in his daily program some form of reading that provides him with the knowledge which he may use in the attainment of his major purpose. Random reading may be pleasant, but it seldom is helpful in connection with one's occupation.

"Reading, however, is not the only source of education. By a careful choice among his daily associates in his occupation, one may ally himself with men from whom he can acquire a liberal education through ordinary conversation.

"Business and professional clubs offer an opportunity for one to form alliances of great educational benefit, provided the man chooses his clubs and his close associates in those clubs with a definite objective in mind. Through this sort of association many men have formed both business and social acquaintances of great value to them in carrying out the object of their major purpose.

"No man can go through life successfully without the habit of cultivating friends. The word 'contact,' as it is commonly used in relationship to personal acquaintanceship, is an important word. If a man makes it a part of his daily practice to extend his list of personal 'contacts' he will find the habit of great benefit to him in ways that cannot be foretold while he is cultivating those acquaintances, but the time will come when they will be ready and willing to render aid to him if he has done a good job of selling himself.

"As I have stated, a man with a Definite Major Purpose should form the habit of establishing 'contacts' through every source possible, using care of course to choose those sources through which he is most likely to meet people who may be helpful to him.

"The church is among the more desirable sources through which one may meet and cultivate people, because it brings people together under circumstances which inspire the spirit of fellowship among men.

"Every man needs some source through which he can associate with his neighbors under circumstances that will enable him to exchange thoughts with them for the sake of mutual understanding and friendship, quite aside from all considerations of pecuniary gain. The man who shuts himself up in his own shell becomes a confirmed introvert, and soon becomes selfish and narrow in his views on life.

Politics

"It is both the duty and the privilege of an American citizen to interest himself in politics and thereby exercise his right to help place, through his ballot, worthy men and women in public office.

"The political party to which a man belongs is of much less importance than the question of his exercising his privilege of voting. If politics become smeared with dishonest practices there is no one to blame but the people who have it within their power to keep dishonest, unworthy and inefficient people out of office.

"In addition to the privilege of voting and the duty it carries with it, one should not overlook the benefits which may be gained from an active interest in politics, through 'contacts' and alliances with people who may become helpful in the attainment of one's Definite Major Purpose.

"In many occupations, professions and businesses, political influence becomes a definite and important factor in the promotion of one's interests. Business and professional men and women certainly should not neglect the possibility of promoting their interests through active political alliances.

"The alert individual, who understands the necessity of reaching out in every possible direction for friendly allies whom he can use in attaining his major purpose in life, will make the fullest use of his privilege of voting.

"But, the major reason why every American citizen

should take an active interest in politics, and the one which I would emphasize above all others, is the fact that if the better type of citizen fails to exercise his right to vote, politics will disintegrate and become an evil that will destroy this nation.

"The founders of this nation pledged their lives and their fortunes to provide all the people with the privileges of liberty and freedom in the pursuit of their chosen purpose in life. And chief among these privileges is that of helping, by the ballot, to maintain the institution of Government which the founders of this nation established to protect those privileges.

"Everything that is worth having has a definite price.

"You desire personal freedom and individual liberty! Very well, you may protect this right by forming a Master Mind alliance with other honest and patriotic men, and making it your business to elect honest men to public office. And it is no exaggeration to state that this may well be the most important Master Mind alliance that any American citizen can make.

"Your forefathers insured your personal liberty and freedom by their votes. *You should do no less for your offspring and the generations that will follow them!*

"Every honest American citizen has sufficient influence with his neighbors, and his daily associates in connection with his occupation, to enable him to influence at least five other people to exercise their right to vote. If he fails to exercise this influence he may still remain an honest citizen, but he cannot truthfully call himself a *patriotic citizen*, for patriotism has a price consisting in the obligation to exercise it.

Social Alliances

"Here is a fertile, almost unlimited, field for the cultivation of friendly 'contacts.' It is particularly available to the married man whose wife understands the art of making friends through social activities.

"Such a wife can convert her home and her social activities into a priceless asset to her husband, if his occupation is one that requires him to extend his list of friends.

"Many professional men whose professional ethics forbid direct advertising or self-promotion, may make effective use of their social privileges, provided they have wives with a bent for social activities.

"A successful life insurance man sells more than a million dollars a year of insurance, with the aid of his wife, who is a member of several Business Women's Clubs. His wife's part is simple. She entertains her fellow club members in her home from time to time, along with their husbands. In this way her husband becomes acquainted with them under friendly circumstances.

"A lawyer's wife has been credited with helping him to build one of the most lucrative law practices in a middle western city, by the simple process of entertaining, through her social activities, the wives of wealthy business men. The possibilities in this direction are endless.

"One of the major advantages of friendly alliances with people in a variety of walks of life consists in the opportunity such contacts provide for 'round-table' discussions which lead to the accumulation of knowledge one may use in the attainment of his Definite Major Purpose.

"If one's acquaintances are sufficiently numerous and varied, they may become a valuable source of information on a wide range of subjects, thus leading to a form of intellectual intercourse which is essential for the development of flexibility and versatility required in many callings.

"When a group of men get together and enter into a round-table discussion on any subject, this sort of spontaneous expression and interchange of thought enriches the minds of all who participate. Every man needs to reinforce his own ideas and plans with new food for thought, which he can acquire only through frank and sincere discussions with people whose experience and education differ from his own.

"The writer who becomes a 'top-notcher' and remains in that exalted position must add continuously to his own stock of knowledge by appropriating the thoughts and ideas of others, through personal contacts and by reading.

"Any mind that remains brilliant, alert, receptive and flexible must be fed continuously from the storehouse of other minds. If this renewal is neglected the mind will atrophy, the same as will an arm that is taken out of use. This is in accordance with nature's laws. Study nature's plan and you will discover that every living thing, from the smallest insect to the complicated machinery of a human being, grows and remains healthy only by constant use.

"Round-table discussions not only add to one's store of useful knowledge, but they develop and expand the power of the mind. The person who stops studying the day he finishes his formal schooling will never become an educated person, no matter how much knowledge he may acquire while he is going to school.

"Life itself is a great school, and everything that inspires thought is a teacher. The wise man knows this; moreover, he makes it a part of his daily routine to contact other minds, with the object of developing his own mind through the exchange of thoughts.

"We see, therefore, that the Master Mind principle has an unlimited scope of practical use. It is the medium by which the individual may supplement the power of his own mind with the knowledge, experience and mental attitude of other minds.

"As one man so aptly expressed this idea: 'If I give you one of my dollars in return for one of yours, each of us will have no more than he started with; but, if I give you a thought in return for one of your thoughts, each of us will have gained a hundred percent dividend on his investment of time.'

"No form of human relationship is as profitable as that through which men exchange useful thoughts, and it may be surprising but true that one may acquire from the mind of the humblest person ideas of the first magnitude of importance.

"Let me illustrate what I mean, through the story of a preacher who picked from the mind of the janitor of his church an idea that led to the attainment of his Definite Major Purpose.

"The preacher's name was Russell Conwell, and his major purpose was the founding of a college he had long desired to establish. All he needed was the necessary money, a tidy sum of something more than a million dollars.

"One day the Reverend Russell Conwell stopped to chat with the janitor who was busily at work cutting the church lawn. As they stood there talking in light conversation, Reverend Conwell casually remarked that the grass adjoining the churchyard was much greener and better kept than their own lawn, intending his remark as a mild reprimand to the old care-taker.

"With a broad grin on his face the janitor replied: 'Yes, that grass sure does look greener, but that's because we're so used to the grass on this side of the fence.'

"Now there was nothing brilliant about that remark, for it was not intended to be anything more than an alibi for laziness, but it planted in the fertile mind of Russell Conwell the seed of an idea—just a bare, tiny seed of thought, mind you—which led to the solution of his major problem.

"From that humble remark an idea was born for a lecture which the preacher composed and delivered more than four thousand times. He called it 'Acres of Diamonds.' The central idea of the lecture was this: A man need not seek his opportunity in the distance, but he can find it right where he stands, by recognizing the fact that the grass on the other side of the fence is no greener than that where he stands.

"The lecture yielded an income during the life of Russell Conwell of more than six million dollars. It was published in book form and became a best seller throughout the nation for many years thereafter, and it may be obtained to this day. The money was used to found and maintain Temple University of Philadelphia, Pennsylvania, one of the great educational institutions of the country.

"The idea around which that lecture was organized did more than found a university. It enriched the minds of millions of people by influencing them to look for opportunity right where they were. The philosophy of the lecture is as sound today as it was when it first came from the mind of a working man.

"Remember his: Every active brain is a potential source of inspiration from which one may procure an idea, or the mere seed of an idea, of priceless value in the solution of his personal problems, or the attainment of his major purpose in life.

"Sometimes great ideas spring from humble minds, but generally they come from the minds of those closest to the individual, where The Master Mind relationship has been deliberately established and maintained.

"The most profitable idea of my own career came one afternoon when Charlie Schwab and I were walking across a golf course. As we finished out shots on the thirteenth hole, Charlie looked up with a sheepish grin on his face, and said,

'I'm three strokes up on you at this hole, Chief; but I have just thought of an idea that should give you a lot of free time to play golf.'

"Curiosity prompted me to inquire as to the nature of the idea. He gave it to me, in one brief sentence, each word of which was worth, roughly speaking, a million dollars. 'Consolidate all your steel plants,' said he, 'into one big corporation and sell it out to Wall Street bankers.'

"Nothing more was said about the matter during the game, but that evening I began to turn the suggestion over in my mind and think about it. Before I went to sleep that night I had converted the seed of his idea into a definite major purpose. The following week I sent Charlie Schwab to New York City to deliver a speech before a group of Wall Street bankers, among them, J. Pierpont Morgan.

"The sum and substance of the speech was a plan for the organization of the United States Steel Corporation, through which I consolidated all my steel plants and retired from active business, with more money than anyone needs.

"Now let me emphasize one point: Charlie Schwab's idea might never have been born, and I never would have received the benefit of it if I had not made it my business to encourage in my associates the creation of new ideas. This encouragement was provided through a close and continuous Master Mind alliance with the members of my business organization, among whom was Charlie Schwab.

"Contact, let me repeat, is an important word!

"It is much more important if we add to it the word 'harmonious!' Through harmonious relationships with the minds of other men an individual may have the full use of his capacity to create ideas. The man who overlooks this great fact thereby condemns himself eternally to penury and want.

"No man is smart enough to project his influence very far into the world without the friendly cooperation of other men. Drive this thought home in every way you can, for it is sufficient unto itself to open the door to success in the higher brackets of individual achievement.

"Too many people look for success in the distance, far from where they are; and altogether too often they search for it through complicated plans based upon a belief in luck or 'miracles' which they hope may favor them.

"As Russell Conwell so effectively stated the matter in his

89

lecture, some people seem to think the grass is greener on the other side of the fence from where they stand, and they pass up the 'Acres of Diamonds' in the form of ideas and opportunities which are available to them through the minds of their daily associates.

"I found my 'Acres of Diamonds' right where I stood, while looking into the glow of a hot steel blast furnace. I remember well the first day I began to sell myself the idea of becoming a leader in the great steel industry instead of remaining a helper in another man's 'Acres of Diamonds.'

"At first the thought was not very definite. It was a wish more than it was a definite purpose. But I began to bring it back into my mind and to encourage it to take possession of me, until there came the day when the idea began to drive me instead of my having to drive it.

"That day I began with earnestness to work my own 'Acres of Diamonds,' and I was surprised to learn how quickly a Definite Major Purpose may find a way to translate itself into its physical equivalent.

"The main thing of importance is to know what one wants.

"The next thing of importance is to begin digging for diamonds right where one is, using whatever tools may be at hand, even if they be only the tools of thought. In proportion to the faithful use a man makes of the tools at hand, other and better tools will be placed in his hands when he is ready for them.

"The man who understands the Master Mind principle and makes use of it will find the necessary tools much more quickly than will the fellow who knows nothing of this principle.

"Every mind needs friendly contact with other minds, for the food of expansion and growth. The discriminating person who has a Definite Major Purpose in life chooses, with the greatest of care, the types of minds with whom he associates most intimately, because he recognizes that he will take on a definite portion of the personality of every person with whom he thus associates.

"I wouldn't give much for a man who does not make it his business to seek the company of people who know more than he. A man rises to the level of his superiors or falls to the level of his inferiors, according to the class he emulates through his choice of associates.

"Lastly, there is one other thought which every man who

90

works for wages or a salary should recognize and respect. It lies in the fact that his job is, and should be, a schooling for a higher station in life, for which he is being paid in two important ways; first, by the wages he receives directly, and secondly, by the experience he gains from his work. And it frequently becomes true that a man's greatest pay consists not in his pay envelope, *but in the experience he gains from his work!*

"This overplus pay a man may gain from his experience depends largely for its value upon the mental attitude in which he relates himself to his associate workers; both those above him and those beneath him. If his attitude is positive and cooperative, and he follows the habit of Going The Extra Mile, his advancement will be both sure and rapid.

"Thus we see that the man who gets ahead not only makes practical use of the principle of the Master Mind, but he also applies the principle of Going The Extra Mile, and the principle of Definiteness of Purpose; the three principles which are inseparably associated with successful men in all walks of life.

Marriage

"Marriage is by far the most important alliance any man ever experiences during his entire life.

"It is important financially, physically, mentally and spiritually, for it is a relationship bound together by all of these.

"The home is the place where most Master Mind alliances should begin, and the man who has chosen his mate wisely will, if he is wise in an economic sense, make his wife the first member of his personal Master Mind group.

"The home alliance should include not only man and wife, but it should include other members of the family if they live in the same household, particularly children.

"The Master Mind principle brings into action the spiritual forces of those who are thus allied for a definite purpose; and spiritual power, while it may seem intangible, is nevertheless the greatest of all powers.

"The married man who is on the right terms with his wife—terms of *complete harmony, understanding, sympathy*

91

and *singleness of purpose* in which each is interested—has a priceless asset in this relationship which may lift him to great heights of personal achievement.

"Inharmony between a man and his wife is unpardonable, no matter what may be the cause. It is unpardonable because it may destroy a man's chances of success, even though he has every attribute necessary for success.

For Wives Only

"And may I here interpolate a suggestion for the benefit of the wives of men?

"The suggestion may, if it is heeded and followed, make just the difference between a lifetime of poverty and misery and a lifetime of opulence and plenty.

"The wife has more influence over her husband than has any other person. That is, she has this superior influence if she has made the most of her relationship to her husband. He chose her in marriage in preference to all other women of his acquaintance, which means that she has his love and his confidence.

"Love heads the list of the nine basic motives of life which inspire all voluntary actions of people. Through the emotion of love the wife may send her husband to his daily labor in a spirit which knows no such reality as failure. But remember that 'nagging,' jealousy, fault-finding and indifference do not feed the emotion of love. They kill it.

"If a wife is wise she will arrange with her husband for a regular Master Mind hour each day; a period during which they will pool all of their mutual interests and discuss them in detail, in a spirit of love and understanding. The periods most suited for this Master Mind talk are those following the morning meal and just before retiring at night.

"And every meal hour should be a period of friendly intercourse between the wife and her husband. They should not be converted into periods of inquisition and fault-finding, but rather should be converted into periods of family worship, during which there will be good cheer, and the discussion of pleasant subjects of mutual interest to the husband and wife.

92

"More family relationships are wrecked at the family meal hour than at any other time, for this is the house which many families devote to settling their family differences of opinion, or to disciplining the children.

"It has been said that a man's stomach is the way to his heart. Therefore the meal hour provides an excellent opportunity for a wife to reach her husband's heart with any idea she desires to plant there. But the approach must be based on love and affection; not upon negative habits of discipline and fault-finding.

"The wife can coax her husband to do many things!

"The wife should take a keen interest in her husband's occupation. She should become familiar with every feature of it, and never overlook an opportunity to express a keen interest in everything that concerns the source from which he earns his livelihood. And above all, she should not be one of those wives who say to their husbands, by inference if not by words, 'You bring home the money and I will spend it, but don't bother me with the details as to how you earn it, for I am not interested in that.'

"If a wife takes that attitude, the time will come when her husband will not be interested as to how much money he brings home, and the time may come when he will not bring it all home!

"I think that wives who are wise will understand just what I mean.

"When a woman marries she becomes the majority stockholder in the firm. If she relates herself to her husband by a true application of the Master Mind principle she will continue, as long as the marriage exists, to vote that stock as she pleases.

"The wife who is wise will manage the firm's business by a carefully prepared budget, taking care not to spend more than the income will allow. Many marriages go on the rocks because the firm runs out of money. And it is no mere axiom to say that when poverty knocks on the front door, love takes to its heels and runs out through the back door. Love, like a beautiful picture, requires the embellishment of an appropriate frame and proper lighting. It requires cultivation and food, just as does the physical body. Love does not thrive on indifference, nagging, fault-finding or domineering by either party.

"Love thrives best where a man and his wife feed it through

93

singleness of purpose. The wife who remembers this may remain forever the most influential person in the life of her husband. The wife who forgets it may see the time when her husband begins to look around for an opportunity 'to trade her in on a newer model,' to use the phraseology of the automobile industry.

"The husband has the responsibility of earning the living, but the wife may have the responsibility of softening the shocks and the resistances which he will meet in connection with his occupation—a responsibility which the wife can discharge by planning a pleasant home-life, through whatever social activities may be fitting to her husband's calling.

"The wife should see to it that the home is the one place where her husband may lay aside his business or occupational cares and enjoy the ecstasies which only the love and affection and understanding of a wife can provide. The wife who follows this policy will be as wise as the sages, and richer—in the ways that count most—than most queens.

"I would also caution a wife against allowing her maternal instinct to supplant her love for her husband, by transferring all of her love and attention to her children. This mistake has wrecked many homes, and it might well wreck any home if the wife neglects to guard against the error so many wives make of switching their love from their husbands to their children.

"A woman's love, if it be the right kind of love, is sufficient in abundance to serve both the children and her husband; and it is a happy wife who sees to it that her love is sufficient to serve her husband and the children generously, without unfair preference in favor of either.

"Where love abounds as the basis of the family Master Mind relationship the family finances will not be likely to give cause for disturbance, for love has a way of surmounting all obstacles, meeting all problems and overcoming all difficulties.

"Family problems may arise, and they do in every family, but love should be the master of them. Keep the light of love shining brightly and everything else will shape itself to the pattern of your most lofty desires.

"I know this counsel is sound as I have followed it in my own family relationship, *and I can truthfully say that it has been responsible for whatever material success I have achieved.*"

(Mr. Carnegie's frank admission becomes impressive when one considers the fact that he accumulated a fortune of more than $500,000,000.00. Mr. Carnegie made a huge fortune, but those who knew of his relationship with his wife know that *Mrs. Carnegie made him!*)

Women Behind the Scene

Taking up the subject of family Master Mind relationships where Andrew Carnegie left it, this seems an appropriate place to call attention to the fact this his experience is by no means an isolated one.

The late Thomas A. Edison freely admitted that Mrs. Edison was the major source of his inspiration. They held their Master Mind meetings daily, usually at the close of Mr. Edison's day's work. And nothing was permitted to interfere with these meetings. Mrs. Edison saw to that, for she recognized the value of her keen interest in all of Mr. Edison's experimental work.

Mr. Edison often worked late into the night, but his homecoming found his wife awaiting him in keen anticipation of hearing him tell of his successes and failures during the day. She was familiar with every experiment he conducted and took an interest in them.

She served as a sort of "sounding board" for Mr. Edison, through whom he had the privilege of looking at his work from the sidelines, and it has been said that she often supplied the missing link to many of his unsolved problems.

If the Master Mind relationship was considered to be of value to men of this caliber, surely it should be regarded as such by men who are struggling to find their places in the world.

The Princes of Love and Romance have played an important role in the lives of all truly great leaders. The story of Robert and Elizabeth Browning is replete with evidence that these unseen entities, which they recognized and respected, were largely responsible for the inspirational literary works of these great poets.

95

John Wanamaker, the Philadelphia "Merchant Prince," as he was known to thousands of people, gave credit to his wife for his rise from poverty to fame and fortune. Master Mind meetings were a part of their daily routine, every evening being set aside in part of these meetings—usually just before they retired.

History attributes the rise to military power of Napoleon Bonaparte to the inspirational influence of his first wife, Josephine. Napoleon's military successes began to wane when he allowed his ambition for power to cause him to put Josephine aside, and his defeat and banishment to the lonely island of St. Helena was not far ahead of this act.

It may not be amiss to mention the fact that many a modern-times business "Napoleon" has met with the same kind of defeat for the same reason. Men often maintain their Master Mind relationships with their wives until they attain power, fame and fortune, then "trade them in for newer models," as Andrew Carnegie expressed it.

Charles M. Schwab's story was different. He too gained fame and fortune through his Master Mind alliance with Andrew Carnegie, aided by a similar relationship with his wife, who was an invalid during the major portion of their married life. He did not put her away on that account, but stood loyally by her until her death, because he believed that loyalty is the first requirement of sound character.

Loyalty

While we are on the subject of loyalty, it may not be out of place to suggest that the lack of loyalty among men in business Master Mind relationships is among the more frequent causes of business failure. As long as associates in business maintain the spirit of loyalty between one another, they generally find a way to bridge their defeats and overcome their handicaps.

It has been said that the first trait of character which Andrew Carnegie looked for in the young men whom he raised from the ranks of his workers to highly paid executive positions, was the trait of loyalty. He often said that if a man did not have inherently the quality of loyalty, he did not

96

have the proper foundation for a sound character in other directions.

His methods of testing men for loyalty were both ingenious and multiple in scope. The testings took place before promotions were made and afterward, until such time as there no longer remained any doubt as to a man's loyalty. And it is a tribute to the deep understanding of men which Mr. Carnegie possessed, that he made but few mistakes in judging men of loyalty.

Do not reveal the purpose of your Master Mind alliance to those outside of the alliance, and make sure that the members of your alliance refrain from so doing, because the idle, the scoffers and the envious stand on the sidelines of life, looking for an opportunity to sow the seeds of discouragement in the minds of those who are excelling them. Avoid this pitfall by keeping your plans to yourself, except insofar as they may be revealed by your actions and achievements.

Do not go into your Master Mind meetings with your mind filled with a negative mental attitude. Remember, if you are the leader of your Master Mind group it is your responsibility to keep every member of the alliance aroused to a high degree of interest and enthusiasm. You cannot do this when you are negative. Moreover, men will not follow with enthusiasm the man who shows a tendency toward doubt, indecision or lack of faith in the object of his Definite Major Purpose. Keep your Master Mind allies keyed up to a high degree of enthusiasm by keeping yourself keyed up in the same manner.

Do not neglect to see that each member of your Master Mind alliance receives adequate compensation, in one form or another, in proportion to the contributions each man makes to your success. Remember that no one ever does anything with enthusiasm unless he benefits thereby. Familiarize yourself with the nine basic motives which inspire all voluntary action, and see that each of your Master Mind allies is properly motivated to give you his loyalty, enthusiasm and complete confidence.

If you are related to your Master Mind allies by the motive of desire for financial gain, be sure that you give more than you receive, by adopting and following the principle of Going

97

the Extra Mile. Do this voluntarily, before you are requested to do so, if you wish to make the most of the habit.

Do not place competitors in your Master Mind alliance, but follow the Rotary Club policy of surrounding yourself with men who have no reason to feel antagonistic toward each other—men who are not in competition with one another.

Do not try to dominate your Master Mind group by force, fear, or coercion, but hold your leadership by diplomacy based upon a definite motive for loyalty and cooperation. The day of leadership by force is gone. Do not try to revive it, for it has no place in civilized life.

Do not fail to take every step necessary to create the spirit of fellowship among your Master Mind allies, for friendly teamwork will give you power attainable in no other way.

The most powerful Master Mind alliance in the history of mankind was formed by the United Nations during World War II. Its leaders announced to the whole world that their Definite Major Purpose was based upon the determination to establish human liberty and freedom for all the peoples of the world, *both the victors and the vanquished alike!*

That pronouncement was worth a thousand victories on the fields of battle, for it had the effect of establishing confidence in the minds of people who were affected by the outcome of that war. Without confidence there can be no Master Mind relationship, either in the field of military operations or elsewhere.

Confidence is the basis of all harmonious relationships. Remember this when you organize your Master Mind alliance if you wish that alliance to endure and to serve your interests effectively.

I have now revealed to you the working principle of the greatest of all the sources of personal power among men—the Master Mind.

By the combination of the first four principles of this philosophy—the Habit of Going the Extra Mile, Definiteness of Purpose, the Master Mind, and the one which follows—one may acquire a clue as to the secret of the power which is available through the Master-Key to Riches.

Therefore, it is not out of place for me to warn you to approach the analysis of our next chapter in a state of expectancy, for it may well mark the most important turning-point of your life.

Analysis of the Master Mind Principle ▪

I shall now reveal to you the true approach to a full understanding of a power which has defied analysis by the entire world of science. Moreover, I shall hope to provide you with the formula by which you may appropriate this power and use it for the attainment of your Definite Major Purpose in life.

Chapter Eight

APPLIED FAITH

Faith is a royal visitor which enters only the mind that has been properly prepared for it; the mind that has been set in order through *self-discipline*.

In the fashion of all royalty, Faith commands the best room; nay, the finest suite, in the mental dwelling place.

It will not be shunted into servant's quarters, and it will not associate with envy, greed, superstition, hatred, revenge, vanity, doubt, worry or fear.

Get the full significance of this truth and you will be on the way to an understanding of that mysterious power which has baffled the scientists down through the ages.

Then you will recognize the necessity for *conditioning your mind*, through self-discipline, before expecting Faith to become your permanent guest.

Recalling the words of the sage of Concord, Ralph Waldo Emerson, who said, "In every man there is something wherein I may learn of him, and in that I am his pupil," I shall now introduce a man who has been a great benefactor of mankind, so that you may observe how one goes about the conditioning of his mind for the expression of Faith.

Let him tell his own story:

"During the business depression which began in 1929 I took a post-graduate course in the University of Hard Knocks, the greatest of all schools.

"It was then I discovered a hidden fortune which I possessed, but had not been using.

"I made the discovery one morning when a notice came that my bank had closed its doors, possibly never to be reopened again, for it was then that I began to take inventory of my intangible, unused assets.

100

"Come with me while I describe what the inventory revealed. Let us begin with the most important item on the list, *unused Faith!*

"When I searched deeply into my own heart I discovered, despite my financial losses, I had an abundance of Faith left in Infinite Intelligence and Faith in my fellowmen.

"With this discovery came another of still greater importance; the discovery that *Faith can accomplish that which not all the money of the world can achieve.*

"When I possessed all the money I needed I made the grievous error of believing money to be a permanent source of power. Now came the astonishing revelation that money, without Faith, is nothing but so much inert matter, *of itself possessed of no power whatsoever.*

"Recognizing, perhaps for the first time in my life, the stupendous power of enduring Faith, I analyzed myself carefully to determine just how much of this form of riches I possessed. The analysis was both surprising and gratifying.

"I began the analysis by taking a walk into the woods. I wished to get away from the crowd, away from the noise of the city, away from the disturbances of civilization and the fears of men, that I might meditate in silence.

"Ah! what gratification there is in that world 'silence'.

"On my journey I picked up an acorn and held it in the palm of my hand. I found it near the roots of the giant oak tree from which it had fallen. I judged the age of the tree to have been so great that it must have been a fair-sized tree when George Washington was but a small boy.

"As I stood there looking at the great tree, and its small embryonic offspring which I held in my hand, I realized that the tree had grown from a small acorn. I also realized that all the men living could not have built such a tree.

"I was conscious of the fact that some form of intangible Intelligence created the acorn from which the tree grew, and caused the acorn to germinate and begin its climb up from the soil of the earth.

"Then I realized that the greatest powers are the intangible powers, and not those which consist in bank balances or material things.

"I picked up a handful of black soil and covered the acorn with it. I held in my hand the *visible portion* of the substance out of which that magnificent tree had grown.

"At the root of the giant oak I plucked a fern. Its leaves

101

were beautifully designed—yes, *designed*—and I realized as I examined the fern that it, too, was created by the same Intelligence which had produced the oak tree.

"I continued my walk in the woods until I came to a running brook of clear, sparkling water. By this time I was tired, so I sat near the brook to rest and listen to its rhythmic music, as it danced on its way back to the sea.

"The experience brought back memories of my youth. I remembered playing by a similar brook. As I sat there listening to the music of the water I became conscious of an unseen being—an Intelligence—which spoke to me from within and told me the enchanting story of the water, and this is the story it told:

" 'Water! Pure sparkling water. The same has been rendering service ever since this planet cooled off and became the home of man, beast and vegetation.

" 'Water! Ah, what a story you could tell if you spoke man's language. You have quenched the thirst of endless millions of earthly wayfarers; fed the flowers; expanded into steam and turned the wheels of man-made machinery, condensing and going back again to your original form. You have cleaned the sewers, washed the pavements, rendered countless services to man and beast, returning always to your source in the seas, there to become purified and start your journey of service once again.

" 'When you move you travel in one direction only, toward the seas from whence you came. You are forever going and coming, but you always seem to be happy at your labor.

" 'Water! Clean, pure, sparkling substance. No matter how much dirty work you perform, you cleanse yourself at the end of your labor.

" 'You cannot be created, nor can you be destroyed. You are akin to all life. Without your beneficence no form of life on this earth would exist!'

"And the water of the brook went rippling, laughing, on its way back to the sea.

"The story of water ended, but I had heard a great sermon; I had been close to the greatest of all forms of Intelligence. I felt evidence of that same Intelligence which had created the great oak tree from a tiny acorn; the Intelligence which had fashioned the leaves of the fern with mechanical and esthetic skill such as no man could duplicate.

"The shadows of the trees were becoming longer; the day was coming to a close.

"As the sun slowly descended beyond the western horizon I realized that it, too, had played a part in that marvelous sermon which I had heard.

"Without the beneficent aid of the sun there could have been no conversion of the acorn into an oak tree. Without the sun's help the sparkling water of the flowing brook would have remained eternally imprisoned in the oceans, and life on this earth could never have existed.

"These thoughts gave a beautiful climax to the sermon I had heard; thoughts of the romantic affinity existing between the sun and the water and all life on this earth, beside which all other forms of romance seemed unimportant.

"I picked up a small white pebble which had been neatly polished by the waters of the running brook. As I held it in my hand I received, from within, a still more impressive sermon. The Intelligence which conveyed that sermon to my mind seemed to say:

" 'Behold, mortal, a miracle which you hold in your hand.

" 'I am only a tiny pebble of stone, yet I am, in reality, a small universe in which there is everything that may be found in the more expanded portion of the universe which you see out there among the stars.

" 'I appear to be dead and motionless, but the appearance is deceiving. I am made of molecules. Inside my molecules are myriads of atoms, each a small universe unto itself. Inside the atoms are countless numbers of electrons which move at an inconceivable rate of speed.

" 'I am not a dead mass of stone, but an organized group of units of ceaseless energy.

" 'I appear to be a solid mass, but the appearance is an illusion, for my electrons are separated one from another by a distance greater than their mass.

" Study me carefully, O humble earthly wayfarer, and remember that the great powers of the universe are the intangibles; that the values of life are those which cannot be added by bank balances.'

"The thought conveyed by that climax was so illuminating that it held me spell-bound, for I recognized that I held in my hand an infinitesimal portion of the energy which keeps the sun, the stars and the earth, on which we live for a brief period, in their respective places in relation to one another.

103

"Meditation revealed to me the beautiful reality that there is law and order, even in the small confines of a tiny pebble of stone. I recognized that within the mass of that tiny pebble the romance and the reality of nature were combined. I recognized that within that small pebble fact transcended fancy.

"Never before had I felt so keenly the significance of the evidence of natural law and order and purpose which reveal themselves in everything the human mind can perceive. Never before had I felt myself so near the source of my Faith in Infinite Intelligence.

"It was a beautiful experience, out there in the midst of Mother Nature's family of trees and running brooks, where the very calmness of the surroundings bade my weary soul be quiet and rest awhile, so that I might look, feel and listen while Infinite Intelligence unfolded to me the story of its reality.

"Never, in all my life, had I previously been so overwhelmingly conscious of the real evidence of Infinite Intelligence, or of the source of my Faith.

"I lingered in this newly found paradise until the Evening Star began to twinkle; then reluctantly I retraced my footsteps back to the city, there to mingle once again with those who are driven, like galley slaves, by the inexorable rules of civilization, in a mad scramble to gather up material things they do not need.

"I am now back in my study, with my books and my typewriter, on which I am recording the story of my experience. But I am swept by a feeling of loneliness and a longing to be out there by the side of that friendly brook where, only a few hours ago, I had bathed my soul in the satisfying realities of Infinite Intelligence.

"I know that my Faith in Infinite Intelligence is real and enduring. It is not a blind Faith; it is one based on close examination of the handiwork of Infinite Intelligence, and as such has been expressed in the orderliness of the universe.

"I had been looking in the wrong direction for the source of my Faith. I had been seeking it in the deeds of men, in human relationships, in bank balances and material things.

"I found it in a tiny acorn, a giant oak tree, a small pebble or stone, the leaves of a simple fern and the soil of the earth; in the friendly sun which warms the earth and gives motion to the waters; in the Evening Star; in the silence and calm of the great outdoors.

104

"And I am moved to suggest that Infinite Intelligence reveals itself through silence more readily than through the boisterousness of men's struggles, in their mad rush to accumulate material things.

"My bank account vanished, my bank collapsed, but I was richer than most millionaires, because I had discovered a direct approach to Faith. With this power behind me I can accumulate other bank balances sufficient for my needs.

"Nay, I am richer than are most millionaires, because I depend upon a source of inspired power which reveals itself to me from within, while many of the more wealthy find it necessary to turn to bank balances and the stock ticker for stimulation and power.

"*My source of power is as free as the air I breathe,* and as *limitless!* To avail myself of it I have only to turn on my Faith, and this I have in abundance.

"Thus, once again I learned the truth that every adversity carries with it the seed of an equivalent benefit. My adversity cost me my bank balance. It paid off through the revelation of the means to all riches!"

Enduring Sources of Faith

Stated in his own words, you have the story of a man who has discovered how to condition his mind for the expression of Faith.

And what a dramatic story it is! *Dramatic because of its simplicity.*

Here is a man who found a sound basis for an enduring Faith; not in bank balances or material riches, but in the seed of an oak tree, the leaves of a fern, a small pebble, and a running brook; things which everyone may observe and appreciate.

But his observation of these simple things led him to recognize that the greatest powers are intangible powers which are revealed through the simple things around us.

I have related this man's story as I wished to emphasize the manner in which one may clear his mind, even in the midst of chaos and insurmountable difficulties, and prepare it for the expression of Faith.

The most important fact which this story reveals is this:

When the mind has been cleared of a *negative mental attitude* the power of Faith moves in and begins to take possession!

Surely no student of this philosophy will be unfortunate enough to miss this important observation.

Let us turn now to an analysis of Faith, although we must approach the subject with full recognition that Faith is a power which has defied analysis by the entire scientific world.

Faith has been given fourth place in this philosophy because it comes near to representing the "fourth dimension," although it is presented here for its relationship to personal achievement.

Faith is a state of mind which might properly be called the "mainspring of the soul" through which one's aims, desires and purposes may be translated into their physical or financial equivalent.

Previously we observed that great power may be attained by the application of (1) the habit of Going the Extra Mile, (2) Definiteness of Purpose, and (3) the Master Mind. But that power is feeble in comparison with that which is available through the combined application of these principles with the state of mind known as Faith.

We have already observed that *capacity for faith* is one of the Twelve Riches. Let us now recognize the means by which this "capacity" may be filled with that strange power which has been the main bulwark of civilization, the chief cause of all human progress, the guiding spirit of all constructive human endeavor.

Let us remember, at the outset of this analysis, that Faith is a state of mind which may be enjoyed only by those who have learned the art of taking *full and complete control* of their minds! This is the one and only prerogative over which an individual has been given complete control.

Faith expresses its powers only through the mind that has been prepared for it. But the way of preparation is known and may be attained by all who desire to find it.

The Fundamentals of Faith are These:

(a) Definiteness of Purpose supported by personal initiative or *action*.

(b) The habit of *going the extra mile* in all human relationships.

(c) A Master Mind alliance with one or more people who radiate courage based on Faith, and who are suited spiritually and mentally to one's needs in carrying out a given purpose.

(d) A positive mind, free from all negatives, such as fear, envy, greed, hatred, jealousy and superstition. (A positive mental attitude is the first and the most important of the Twelve Riches.)

(e) Recognition of the truth that every adversity carries with it the seed of an equivalent benefit; *that temporary defeat is not failure* until it has been accepted as such.

(f) The habit of affirming one's Definite Major Purpose in life, in a ceremony of meditation, at least once daily.

(g) Recognition of the existence of Infinite Intelligence which gives orderliness to the universe; that all individuals are minute expressions of this Intelligence, and as such the individual mind has no limitations except those which are accepted and set up by the individual in his own mind.

(h) A careful inventory (in retrospect) of one's past defeats and adversities, which will reveal the truth that all such experiences carry the seed of an equivalent benefit.

(i) Self-respect expressed through harmony with one's own conscience.

(j) Recognition of the oneness of all mankind.

These are the fundamentals of major importance which prepare the mind for the expression of Faith. Their application calls for no degree of superiority, but application does call for intelligence and *a keen thirst for truth and justice.*

Faith fraternizes only with the mind that is positive!

It is the *"elan vital"* that gives power, inspiration and action to a positive mind. It is the power that causes a positive mind to act as an "electro-magnet," attracting to it the exact physical counterpart of the thought it expresses.

Faith gives resourcefulness to the mind, enabling the mind to make "grist of all that comes to its mill." It recognizes favorable opportunities, in every circumstance of one's life, whereby one may attain the object of Faith, *going so far as to provide the means by which failure and defeat may be converted into success of equivalent dimensions.*

Faith enables man to penetrate deeply into the secrets of

107

Nature and to understand Nature's language as it is expressed in all natural laws.

From this sort of revelation have come all the great inventions that serve mankind, and a better understanding of the way to human freedom through harmony in human relationships.

Faith makes it possible to achieve that which man can *conceive* and *believe!*

Thomas A. Edison *believed* he could perfect a practical incandescent electric lamp, and despite the fact that he failed more than 10,000 times that Faith carried him to the discovery of the secret for which he was searching.

Signor Marconi *believed* the energy of the ether could be made to carry the vibrations of sound without the use of wires. His Faith carried him through endless failures until at long last he was rewarded by triumph.

Christopher Columbus *believed* the earth was round; that he would find land in an uncharted ocean if he sailed on. Despite the rebellious protests of his *unbelieving* sailors he sailed on and on until he was rewarded for his Faith.

Helen Keller *believed* she would learn to speak, although she had lost the power of speech, her hearing, and her eyesight as well. Her Faith restored her speech and provided her with the equivalent of hearing, through the sense of touch, thus proving that Faith can and will find a way to the realization of human desires.

If you would have Faith, keep your mind on that which you desire. And remember that there is no such reality as a "blanket" faith, for faith is the outward demonstration of definiteness of purpose.

Faith is guidance from within! The guiding force is Infinite Intelligence directed to definite ends. It will not bring that which one desires, but it will guide one to the attainment of the object of desire.

How to Demonstrate the Power of Faith

(a) Know what you want and determine what you have to give in return for it.

(b) When you affirm the objects of your desires, through prayer, inspire your imagination to see yourself already in

108

possession of them, and act precisely as if you were in the physical possession thereof. (Remember, the possession of anything first takes place mentally, in the mind.)

(c) Keep the mind open at all times for *guidance from within*, and when you are inspired by "hunches" to modify your plans or to move on a new plan, move without hesitancy or doubt.

(d) When overtaken by temporary defeat, as you may be overtaken many times, remember that man's Faith is tested in many ways, and your defeat may be only one of your "testing periods." Therefore, accept defeat as an inspiration to greater effort and carry on with *belief* that you will succeed.

(e) Any negative state of mind will destroy the capacity for Faith and result in a negative climax of any affirmation you may express. Your state of mind is everything; therefore take possession of your mind and clear it completely of all unwanted interlopers that are unfriendly to Faith, and keep it cleared, no matter what may be the cost in effort.

(f) Learn to give expression to your power of Faith by writing out a clear description of your Definite Major Purpose in life and using it as the basis of your daily meditation.

(g) Associate with your Definite Major Purpose as many as possible of the nine basic motives, described in Chapter One.

(h) Write out a list of all the benefits and advantages you expect to derive from the attainment of the object and your Definite Major Purpose and call these into your mind many times daily, thereby making your mind "success conscious." (This is commonly called auto-suggestion.)

(i) Associate yourself, as far as possible, with people who are in sympathy with your Definite Major Purpose; people who are in harmony with you, and inspire them to encourage you in every way possible.

(j) Let not a single day pass without making at least one definite move toward the attainment of your Definite Major Purpose. Remember, "Faith without works is dead."

(k) Choose some prosperous person of self-reliance and courage as your "pace-maker," and make up your mind not only to keep up with that person, but to excel him. Do this silently, without mentioning your plan to anyone. (Boastfulness will be fatal to your success, as Faith has nothing in common with vanity or self-love.)

(l) Surround yourself with books, pictures, wall mottoes and other suggestive reminders of self-reliance founded upon Faith as it has been demonstrated by other people, thus building around yourself an atmosphere of prosperity and achievement. This habit will be fruitful of stupendous results.

(m) Adopt a policy of never evading or running away from unpleasant circumstances, but recognize such circumstances and build a counter-fire against them right where they overtake you. You will discover that recognition of such circumstances, without fear of their consequence, is nine-tenths of the battle in mastering them.

(n) Recognize the truth that everything worth having has a definite price. The price of Faith, among other things, is eternal vigilance in carrying out these simple instructions. Your watchword must be *persistence*!

These are the steps that lead to the development and the maintenance of a *positive mental attitude*, the only one in which Faith will abide. They are steps that lead to riches of both mind and spirit as well as riches of the purse. Fill your mind with this kind of mental food.

These are the steps by which the mind may be prepared for the highest expressions of the soul.

Faith in Action

Feed your mind on such mental food and it will be easy for you to adopt the habit of *going the extra mile*.

It will be easy for you to keep your mind attuned to that which you desire, with assurance that it shall become yours.

"The key to every man," said Emerson, "is his thought."

That is true. Every man today is the result of his thoughts of yesterday!

James J. Hill sat with his hand on a telegraph key, waiting for an "open line." But he was not idle. His imagination was at work, building a great Transcontinental Railway System through which he hoped to tap the vast resources of the undeveloped western portion of the United States.

He had no money. He had no influential friends. He had no record of great achievement to give him prestige. But he did have Faith, that irresistible power that recognizes no such reality as "impossible."

110

He reduced his Definite Major Purpose to writing, omitting no detail.

On a map of the United States he sketched the course of his proposed railroad.

He slept with that map under his pillow. He carried it with him wherever he went. He fed his mind on his desire for the fulfillment of his "dream" until he made that dream a reality.

The morning after the great Chicago fire had laid waste the business portion of the city, Marshall Field came down to the site where, the day before, his retail store stood.

All around him were groups of other merchants whose stores had also been destroyed. He listened in on their conversations and learned that they had given up hope and many of them had already decided to move on further West and start over again.

Calling the nearest groups to him Mr. Field said:

"Gentlemen, you may do as you please, but as for me I intend to stay right here. Over there where you see the smoking remains of what was once my store I shall build the world's greatest retail store."

The store that Mr. Field built on Faith still stands on that spot, in Chicago.

These men and others like them have been the pioneers who produced our great American way of life.

They gave us our system of railroads and our system of communications.

They gave us the talking pictures; the talking machines; the airplanes; the skyscrapers skeletoned with steel; the automobile; the improved highways; the household electrical appliances; the electric power installations; the x-ray; the banking and investment institutions; the great life insurance companies; yes, and more important than all these, they prepared the way, through their Faith, for the freedom each and every one of us enjoys as an American citizen.

Human progress is no matter of accident or luck!

But it is the result of *applied faith*, expressed by men who have conditioned their minds, through the seventeen principles of this philosophy, for the expression of Faith.

The space that every man occupies in the world is measured by the Faith he expresses in connection with his aims and purposes.

Let us remember this, we who aspire to enjoy freedom and riches.

Let us remember, too, that Faith fixes no limitations of freedom or riches, but it guides every man to the realization of his desires whether they be great or small, according to his expression of it.

And though Faith is the one power which defies the scientists to analyze it, the procedure by which it may be applied is simple and within the understanding of the humblest, thus it is the common property of all mankind.

All that is known of this procedure has been simply stated in this chapter, and not a single step of it is beyond the reach of the humblest person.

Faith begins with *definiteness of purpose* functioning in a mind that has been prepared for it by the development of a *positive mental attitude*. It attains its greatest scope of power by *physical action* directed toward the attainment of a definite purpose.

All voluntary physical action is inspired by one or more of the nine basic motives. It is not difficult for one to develop Faith in connection with the pursuit of one's desires.

Let a man be motivated by *love* and see how quickly this emotion is given wings for action through Faith. And action in pursuit of the objective of that love quickly follows. The action becomes a labor of love, which is one of the Twelve Riches.

Let a man set his heart upon the accumulation of material riches and see how quickly his every effort becomes a labor of love. The hours of the day are not long enough for his needs, and though he labors long he finds that fatigue is softened by the joy of *self-expression*, which is another of the Twelve Riches.

Thus, one by one the resistances of life fade into nothingness for the man who has prepared his mind for self-expression through Faith. Success becomes inevitable. Joy crowns his every effort. He has no time or inclination for hatred. *Harmony in human relationships* comes naturally to him. His *hope of achievement* is high and continuous, for he sees himself already in possession of the object of his definite purpose. Intolerance has been supplanted by an *open mind*.

And *self-discipline* becomes as natural as the eating of food. He *understands people* because he loves them, and because of this love he is willing to *share his blessings. Of fear he knows nothing,* for all his fears have been driven away by his Faith. The Twelve Riches have become his own!

112

Faith is an expression of gratitude for man's relationship to his Creator. Fear is an acknowledgment of the influences of evil and it connotes a lack of *belief* in the Creator.

The greatest of life's riches consist in the understanding of the four principles which I have mentioned. These principles are known as the "Big Four" of this philosophy, because they are the warp and the woof and the major foundation-stones of the Master-Key to the power of thought and the inner secrets of the soul.

Use this Master-Key wisely and you shall be free!

Some to Whom the Master-Key Has Been Revealed

In a one-room log cabin, in Kentucky, a small boy was lying on the hearth, learning to write, using the back of a wooden shovel as a slate, and a piece of charcoal as a pencil.

A kindly woman stood over him, encouraging him to keep on trying. The woman was his mother! The boy grew into manhood without having shown any promise of greatness.

He took up the study of law and tried to make a living at that profession, but his success was meager.

He tried store-keeping, but the sheriff soon caught up with him.

He entered the army, but he made no noteworthy record there. Everything to which he turned his hand seemed to wither and disappear into nothingness.

Then a great love came into his life. It ended with the death of the woman he loved, but the sorrow over that death reached deeply into the man's soul and there it made contact with the *secret power* that comes from within.

He seized that power and began to put it to work. It made him President of the United States. It wiped out the curse of slavery in America. And it saved the Union from dissolution in the time of a great national emergency.

The Great Emancipator is now a citizen of the universe but the spirit of this great soul—a spirit that was set free by the secret power from within his own mind—goes marching on.

So, this power that comes to men from within knows no social caste! It is as available to the poor and the humble as it is to

113

the rich and the powerful. It need not be passed on from one person to another. It is possessed by all who think. It cannot be put into effect for you by any one except yourself. It must be acquired from within, and it is free to all who will appropriate it.

What strange fear is it that gets into the minds of men and short-circuits their approach to this secret power from within, and when it is recognized and used lifts men to great heights of achievement? How and why do the vast majority of the people of the world become the victims of a hypnotic rhythm which destroys their capacity to use the secret power of their own minds? How can this rhythm be broken?

"How may one tap that secret power that comes from within?" some will wish to ask! Let us see how others have drawn upon it.

A young clergyman by the name of Frank Gunsaulus had long desired to build a new type of college. He knew exactly what he wanted, but the hitch came in the fact that it required a million dollars in cash.

He made up his mind to get the million dollars! Definiteness of decision, based upon definiteness of purpose, constituted the first step of his plan.

Then he wrote a sermon entitled "What I Would Do With a Million Dollars!" and announced in the newspapers that he would preach on that subject the following Sunday morning.

At the end of the sermon a strange man whom the young preacher had never seen before arose, walked down to the pulpit, extended his hand and said, "I like your sermon, and you may come down to my office tomorrow morning and I will give you the million dollars you desire."

The man was Philip D. Armour, the packing-house founder of Armour & Company. His gift was the beginning of the Armour School of Technology, one of the great schools of the country.

This is the sum and the substance of what happened. What went on in the mind of the young preacher, that enabled him to contact the secret power that is available through the mind of man, is something with which we can only conjecture, but the modus operandi by which that power was stimulated was *applied Faith!*

Shortly after birth Helen Keller was stricken by a physical affliction which deprived her of sight, hearing and speech. With two of the more important of the five physical senses

114

stilled forever she faced life under difficulties such as most people never know throughout their lives.

With the aid of a kindly woman who recognized the existence of that secret power which comes from within, Helen Keller began to contact that power and use it. In her own words, she gives a definite clue as to one of the conditions under which the power may be revealed.

"Faith," said Miss Keller, "rightly understood, is *active* not *passive!* Passive faith is no more a force than sight is in an eye that does not look or search out. Active faith knows no fear. It denies that God has betrayed His creatures and given the world over to darkness. It denies despair. Reinforced with faith, the weakest mortal is mightier than disaster."

Faith, *backed by action,* was the instrument with which Miss Keller bridged her affliction so that she was restored to a useful life.

A Source of Secret Power

Go back through the pages of history and you will observe that the story of civilization's unfoldment leads inevitably to the works of men and women who opened the door to that secret power from within, with *applied faith* as the master-key! Observe, too, that great achievements always are born of hardship and struggle and barriers which seem insurmountable; obstacles which yield to nothing but *an indomitable will backed by an abiding faith!*

And here, in one short phrase—*indomitable will backed by an abiding faith*—you have the approach of major importance that leads to the discovery of the door of the mind, behind which the secret power from within is hidden!

Men who penetrate that secret power and apply it in the solution of personal problems sometimes are called "dreamers!" But, observe that they back their dreams with action.

When Henry J. Kaiser was building the great Hoover Dam, in Nevada, he sublet a portion of his grading work to Robert G. LeTourneau. Everything moved smoothly for the first few weeks and it looked as if everyone was going to make a lot of money.

Then, as often happens in the lives of men, the streak of

115

good fortune played out when the equipment struck a deep layer of hard granite which was not supposed to exist.

LeTourneau went right ahead with his contract, hoping that the layer of hard stone would not be too thick, giving the job everything he had until he ran out of money.

Meanwhile he had tested the depth of the stone with deep drilling and discovered that it was too much for him, so he reluctantly admitted that he was temporarily defeated.

His friends begged him to go through bankruptcy so he could make a new start in some other field of business.

"No," he exclaimed, "I lost my money in dirt and I will make it back from dirt, and when I do I will pay off every cent I owe."

In that brief sentence LeTourneau expressed about everything worthy of mention that any success philosophy can provide. He expressed definiteness of purpose and faith in his ability to translate that purpose into victory despite his defeat.

"In my hour of greatest distress," said LeTourneau, "I found my greatest asset in the form of a new partner. I took this partner into business with me. I did the muscle work and my partner told me how to do it. His name is God."

His partner sent him into strange places to find the means with which to make a new start. With his wife's curtain rods and some pieces of discarded automobile parts he built his first dirt scraper, with the badly used motor serving to supply the power. The thing worked but it was not large enough to justify its use, so LeTourneau scratched through an automobile "graveyard" until he found better parts and built a second machine. This one did much better than the first but it was still far short of being suitable for commercial use.

"What shall I do now, partner?" LeTourneau asked of the senior member of his firm. And he got the answer swiftly. "Borrow the money you need and build a real machine with new materials."

LeTourneau did just that. From that moment on he began to ride the success beam onward to fame and fortune. He had found that "seed of an equivalent benefit" that came with his loss in Nevada, and he germinated it into the full-blown flower of success.

First, he built a plant in Peoria, Illinois, where his dirt removing equipment was produced in quantity. Next he built a similar plant in Toccoa, Georgia. Not satisfied he built another

116

large plant in Vicksburg, Mississippi, and later another in Longview, Texas.

I was associated with Mr. LeTourneau for eighteen months, mainly for the purpose of finding out at first hand what made him "tick." I was willing to accept Mr. LeTourneau's claim that his success was due to his partnership with God, but I wanted to learn *how and when* the great industrialist contacted his senior partner.

One night when LeTourneau and I were returning to Toccoa from a speaking engagement in LeTourneau's private plane, the secret he had been seeking was revealed. Shortly after the plane took off LeTourneau flopped himself on a couch and in a few minutes he was sound asleep and snoring. In about thirty minutes he raised himself up on his elbow, took a little book from his pocket and wrote several lines in it. Meanwhile he was looking out into space instead of in the notebook.

This happened three different times before the plane reached Toccoa. After the plane landed I asked LeTourneau if he remembered making notes in his notebook.

"Why no!" exclaimed LeTourneau. "Did I make notes?"

He pulled the book from his pocket, looked at it a few seconds, then said, "There it is! There it is! I have been waiting for this for more than a month. There it is! The very information I had to have before I could go ahead."

We got into a car and drove directly to LeTourneau's home. Not a word was spoken on the way.

Regardless of what one may think of Mr. LeTourneau's claim of partnership with the Creator, two facts stand out boldly and they cannot be brushed aside because of what anyone believes or does not believe.

First, he failed in business and lost all of his money under circumstances which might have discouraged the average person from trying the same line of work again.

Secondly, he made a comeback, and despite his almost total lack of formal education he became one of the very rich and successful industrialists of America.

As to *how and when* LeTourneau contacted his senior partner, I got the answer I was seeking. The contact was made through LeTourneau's subconscious mind, where he had carefully etched a clear picture of what he wanted and backed it with absolute *faith* that he would get it in due time.

117

There is nothing new about the system. And it may be applied by anyone who makes use of definiteness of purpose and applied faith as intensely as LeTourneau did.

One of the strange features of "faith, rightly understood," is that it generally appears because of some emergency which forces men to look beyond the power of ordinary thought for the solution of their problems.

It is during these emergencies that we draw upon that secret power from within which knows no resistance strong enough to defeat it. Such emergencies, for example, as that faced by the fifty-six men who gave birth to this nation when they signed their names to the Declaration of Independence.

That was "active faith, rightly understood!" for each man who signed that document knew that it might become his own death-warrant! Fortunately it became a license to liberty for all mankind claiming its protection, and it may well prove yet to be a license to liberty for the entire world.

The benefits of the document were proportionate to the risk assumed by those who signed it. The signers pledged their lives, their fortunes and their rights to liberty, the greatest privileges of a civilized people, and they made the pledge without mental reservations.

A Test of Faith

Here, then, is the suggestion of a test by which men may measure their capacity for *active faith!* To be effective it must be based on a willingness to risk whatever the circumstances demand; liberty, material fortune, and life itself. Faith without risk is a passive faith which, as Helen Keller stated, "is no more a force than sight is in an eye that does not look or search out."

And let us examine the records of some of the great leaders who came after the signers of the Declaration of Independence, for theirs was also an active faith.

They, too, discovered that secret power that comes from within, drew upon it, applied it and converted a vast wilderness into the "cradle of democracy."

Such men as James J. Hill, who pushed back the frontiers of the West and brought the Atlantic and Pacific Oceans into easy access of the people, through a great transcontinental railroad system.

And Lee De Forest, who perfected the mechanical means by which the boundless force of the ether has been harnessed and made to serve as a means of instantaneous communication between the peoples of the world, through the radio.

And Thomas A. Edison, who pushed civilization ahead by thousands of years, with the perfection of the incandescent electric lamp, the talking machine, the moving picture and scores of other useful inventions which lighten the burdens of mankind and add to his pleasure and education.

These, and others of their type, were men of *active faith!* We sometimes call them "geniuses," but they disclaimed the right to the honor because they recognized that their achievements came as the result of that secret power from within which is available to everyone who will embrace it and use it.

We all know of the achievements of these great leaders; we know the rules of their leadership; we recognize the nature and the scope of the blessings their labors have conferred upon the people of this nation, and we have preserved for the people the philosophy of individual achievement through which these men helped to make this the world's richest and freest country.

But, unfortunately, not all of us recognize the handicaps under which they worked, the obstacles they had to overcome, and the spirit of *active faith* in which they carried on their work.

Of this we may be sure, however: *Their achievements were in exact proportion to the emergencies they had to overcome!*

They met with opposition from those who were destined to benefit most by their struggles; people who, because of the lack of *active faith*, always view with skepticism and doubt that which is new and unfamiliar.

The emergencies of life often bring men to the crossroads, where they are forced to choose their direction, one road being marked Faith and another Fear!

What is it that causes the vast majority to take the Fear road? The choice hinges upon one's *mental attitude!*

The man who takes the Faith road is the man who has conditioned his mind to believe; conditioned it a little at a time, by prompt and courageous decisions in the details of his daily experiences. The man who takes the Fear road does so because he has neglected to condition his mind to be positive.

119

In Washington, a man sits in a wheel chair with a tin cup and a bunch of pencils in his hands, gaining a meager living by begging. The *excuse* for his begging is that he lost the use of his legs, through infantile paralysis. His brain has not been affected. He is otherwise strong and healthy. But, his choice led him to accept the Fear road when the dreaded disease overtook him, and his mind atrophies through disuse.

In another part of the same city was another man who was afflicted with the same handicap. He, too, had lost the use of his legs, but his reaction to his loss was far different. When he came to the cross-roads at which he was forced to make a choice he took the Faith road, and it led straight to the White House and the highest position within the gift of the American people.

That which he lost through incapacity of his limbs, he gained in the use of his brain and his will, and it is a matter of record that his physical affliction did in no way hinder him from being one of the most active men who ever occupied the position of President.

The difference in the stations of these two men was very great! But, let no one be deceived as to the cause of this difference, for it is entirely a difference of *mental attitudes*. One man chose Fear as his guide. The other chose Faith.

And, when you come right down to the circumstances which lift some men to high stations in life and condemn others to penury and want, the likelihood is that their widely separated positions reflect their respective mental attitudes. The high man chooses the high road of Faith, the low man chooses the low road of Fear, and education, experience, and personal skill are matters of secondary importance.

When Thomas A. Edison's teacher sent him home from school, at the end of the first three months, with a note to his parents saying he had an "addled" mind and could not be taught, he had the best of excuses for becoming an outcast, a do-nothing, a nobody, and that is precisely what he proceeded to become for a time. He did odd jobs, sold newspapers, tinkered with gadgets and chemicals until he became what is commonly known as a "jack of all trades" and not very good at any.

Then something took place in the mind of Thomas A. Edison that was destined to make his name immortal. Through some strange process which he never fully disclosed to the

120

world, he discovered that secret power from within, took possession of it, organized it and lo! instead of being a man with an "addled" brain he became the outstanding genius of invention.

And now, wherever we see an electric light, or hear a phonograph, or see a moving picture we should be reminded that we are observing the product of that secret power from within which is as available to us as it was to the great Edison. Moreover, we should feel sorely ashamed if, by neglect or indifference, we are making no appropriate use of this great power.

The Power Within

One of the strange features of this secret power from within is that it aids men in procuring whatever they set their hearts upon, which is but another way of saying it translates into reality one's dominating thoughts.

In the little town of Tyler, Texas, a boy still in his 'teens walked into a grocery store where some loafers were sitting by a stove. One of the men looked at the youth, grinned broadly and said, "Say, Sonny, what are you going to be when you are a man?"

"I'll tell you what I'm going to be," the boy answered. "I'm going to be the best lawyer in the world—that's what I'm going to be if you wish to know."

The loafers yelled with laughter! The boy picked up his groceries and quietly walked out of the store.

Later, when the loafers laughed, it was in a different vein, for that boy had become a recognized authority in the legal world and his skill at law was so great that he was earning more than the President of the United States.

His name was Martin W. Littleton. He, too, discovered the secret power within his own mind and that power enabled him to set his own price on his services and get it.

As far as knowledge of the law is concerned there are thousands of lawyers who perhaps are as skilled at law as Martin W. Littleton, but few of them are making more than a living from their profession because they have not discovered there is something that brings success in the legal profession which is not taught in law schools.

121

The illustration might be extended to cover every profession and all human endeavor. In every calling there are a few who rise to the top while all around them are others who never get beyond mediocrity.

Those who succeed usually are called "lucky." To be sure they are lucky! But, learn the facts and you will discover that their "luck" consists of that secret power from within, which they have applied through a *positive mental attitude*; a determination to follow the road of Faith instead of the road of Fear and self-limitation.

The power that comes from within recognizes no such reality as permanent barriers.

It converts defeat into a challenge to greater effort.

It removes self-imposed limitations such as fear and doubt.

And, above all else, let us remember that it makes no black marks against any man's record which he cannot erase.

If approached through the power from within, every day brings forth a newly-born opportunity for individual achievement which need not in any way whatsoever be burdened by the failures of yesterday.

It favors no race or creed, and it is bound by no sort of arbitrary consistency compelling man to remain in poverty because he was born in poverty.

The power from within is the one medium through which the effects of Cosmic Habitforce may be changed from a negative to a positive application instantaneously.

It recognizes no precedent, follows no hard and fast rules, and makes royal kings of the humblest of men at will—their will!

It offers the one and only grand highway to personal freedom and liberty.

It restores health where all else fails, in open defiance of all the rules of modern medical science.

It heals the wounds of sorrow and disappointment regardless of their cause.

It transcends all human experience, all education, all knowledge available to mankind.

And its only fixed price is that of an unyielding faith!—an active applied faith!

It was the inspiration of the poet who wrote:

"Isn't it strange that princes and kings
And clowns that caper in saw-dust rings;

122

And common folks, like you and me,
All are builders for eternity.

"To each is given a book of rules,
A block of stone and a bag of tools;
And each must shape ere time has flown,
A stumbling block or a stepping stone."

Search until you find the point of approach to that secret power from within, and when you find it you will have discovered your true self—that "other self" which makes use of every experience of life.

Then, whether you build a better mouse trap, or write a better book, or preach a better sermon, the world will make a beaten path to your door, recognize you and adequately reward you, no matter who you are or what may have been the nature and scope of your failures of the past.

What if you have failed in the past?

So, at one time, did every man we recognize as a towering success. They all met with failure in one way or another, but they didn't call it by that name; they called it *"temporary defeat."*

With the aid of the light that shines from within, all truly great men have recognized temporary defeat for exactly what it is—*a challenge to greater effort backed by greater faith!*

Anyone can quit when the going is hard!

Anyone can feel sorry for himself when temporary defeat overtakes him, but self-coddling was no part of the character of the men whom the world has recognized as great.

The approach to that power from within cannot be made by self-pity. It cannot be made through fear and timidity. It cannot be made through envy and hatred. It cannot be made through avarice and greed.

No; your "other self" pays no heed to any of these negatives! It manifests itself only through the mind that has been swept clean of all negative mental attitudes. *It thrives in the mind that is guided by faith!*

123

Up From Failure

Lee Braxton, of Whiteville, North Carolina, admits that he became acquainted with poverty early in life, and by hard struggle he managed to get through the sixth grade in school.

He was the tenth child in a family of twelve, and he was forced to begin at a very early age to shift for himself. His father was a village blacksmith. He shined shoes, delivered groceries, sold newspapers, worked in a hosiery mill, washed automobiles, served as a mechanic's helper, and worked his way up to become shop foreman.

He fought hard for every inch of ground he covered until at long last he married, owned a home of his own, and had an income sufficient to provide a modest living for himself and his family.

Then misfortune struck him hard. His income was shut off and his home was advertised for sale to satisfy a mortgage. He lost everything he owned except the most important of his assets—his will to make a new start and his faith in his ability to convert his misfortune into an advantage.

He began at once to look for that "seed of an equivalent benefit" which came with his temporary defeat, and he found it in *Think and Grow Rich*. Someone gave him a copy of this book. Before he had finished reading it through his mental attitude began to change from negative to positive. By the time he finished it he had formed a plan for a comeback and he began immediately to put it into operation.

Through the pages of this book Lee Braxton was introduced to the most important person living—his "other self." That self which he had not known previously. The self that recognized temporary defeat, but failure, never!

From the day of this discovery of his real self everything Lee Braxton touched turned into gold or something finer than gold. He organized the First National Bank of Whiteville and became its first president. Then he promoted and built Whiteville's finest hotel, a modern structure that would be a credit to any city. He organized a company for the financing of automobiles, and a company to sell and distribute automobile parts as well as an automobile sales agency. Then he organized and

124

promoted a retail musical instruments store, and built and paid for one of the finest homes in Whiteville.

The people of Whiteville elected him as mayor of the city and it was said that there was scarcely a single business or profession in the city which had not recognized some form of benefit from his influence and business operations.

His Ship of Fortune was sailing so smoothly that he made up his mind to accumulate as much money as he needed and retire from business by the time he reached the age of fifty. He made it at the age of forty-four, sold out all of his business interests and began contributing his services, free of charge, to a well-known evangelist, in the capacity of radio and television manager. In a very short time he had this evangelist's daily program going on hundreds of radio and television stations in almost every portion of the United States.

Despite his generous praise of *Think and Grow Rich*, it seems but fair to mention that Lee Braxton had the essentials of success before he ever read the book, just as you and every reader of this story have all of the essentials for success of any proportion and nature you desire.

The book took his mind away from his misfortune and gave it an opportunity to reveal to Lee the hidden riches he possessed in the power of his own mind. A power which can be transmuted into any material thing one desires. The book informed Lee Braxton of this irresistible force that dwelled within his brain. He recognized the existence of that power, embraced it and directed it to ends of his own choice.

And that is about all there is to any success story.

When PMA (positive mental attitude) takes over, success is just around the corner and defeat is nothing more than an experience with which one may motivate himself for greater effort. Lee Braxton learned this truth and profited by it. And because he did something about what he learned he placed himself in a position where he could truthfully say "there is no material thing under the sun which I desire that I cannot acquire."

He made Life pay off on his own terms, engaged in the sort of work he liked best and found peace of mind.

It is not a new philosophy of achievement that the world needs!

But it is a re-dedication of the old and tried principles which lead unerringly to the discovery of that power from within which "moves mountains."

The power that has brought forth great leaders in every walk of life and in every generation is still available. Men of vision and faith, who have pushed back the frontiers of ignorance and superstition and fear, have given the world all that we know as civilization.

The power is clothed in no mystery and it performs no miracles, but it works through the daily deeds of men, and reflects itself in every form of service rendered for the benefit of mankind.

It is called by myriad names, but its nature never changes, no matter by what name it is known.

It works through but one medium, and that is the mind.

It expresses itself in thoughts, ideas, plans and purposes of men, and the grandest thing to be said about it is that *it is as free as the air we breathe and as abundant as the scope and space of the universe.*

Chapter Nine

THE LAW OF COSMIC HABITFORCE

Habit is a cable; we weave a thread of it every day, and at last we cannot break it.

—*Horace Mann.*

So, we come now to the analysis of the greatest of all of Nature's laws, the law of Cosmic Habitforce!

Briefly described, the law of Cosmic Habitforce is Nature's method of giving fixation to all habits so that they may carry on automatically once they have been set into motion—the habits of men the same as the habits of the universe.

Every man is where he is and what he is because of his established habits of thoughts and deeds. The purpose of this entire philosophy is to aid the individual in the formation of the kind of habits that will transfer him from where he is to where he wishes to be in life.

Every scientist, and many laymen, know that Nature maintains a perfect balance between all the elements of matter and energy throughout the universe; that the entire universe is operated through an inexorable system of orderliness and habits which never vary, and cannot be altered by any form of human endeavor; that the five known realities of the universe are (1) Time, (2) Space, (3) Energy, (4) Matter, and (5) Intelligence, which shapes the other known realities into orderliness and system based upon *fixed habits*.

These are Nature's building-blocks with which she creates a grain of sand or the largest stars that float through space, and every other thing known to man, or that the mind of man can conceive.

These are the known realities, but not every one has taken

127

the time or the interest to ascertain the fact that Cosmic Habitforce is the particular application of Energy with which Nature maintains the relationship between the atoms of matter, the stars and the planets in their ceaseless motion onward toward some unknown destiny, the seasons of the year, night and day, sickness and health, life and death. Cosmic Habitforce is the medium through which all habits and all human relationships are maintained in varying degrees of permanence, and the medium through which thought is translated into its physical equivalent in response to the desires and purposes of individuals.

But these are truths capable of proof, and one may count that hour sacred during which he discovers the unescapable truth that man is only an instrument through which higher powers than his own are projecting themselves. This entire philosophy is designed to lead one to this important discovery, and to enable him to make use of the knowledge it reveals, *by placing himself in harmony with the unseen forces of the universe which may carry him inevitably into the success side of the great River of Life.*

The hour of this discovery should bring him within easy reach of the Master-Key to all Riches!

Cosmic Habitforce is Nature's Comptroller through which all other natural laws are co-ordinated, organized and operated through orderliness and system. Therefore it is the greatest of all natural laws.

We see the stars and the planets move with such precision that the astronomers can predetermine their exact location and their relationship to one another scores of years hence.

We see the seasons of the year come and go with a clock-like regularity.

We know that an oak tree grows from an acorn, and a pine tree grows from the seed of its ancestor; that an acorn never makes a mistake and produces a pine tree, nor does a pine seed produce an oak tree. We know that nothing is ever produced that does not have its antecedents in something similar which preceded it, that the nature and the purpose of one's thoughts produce fruits after their kind, just as surely as fire produces smoke.

Cosmic Habitforce is the medium by which every living thing is forced to take on and become a part of the environmental influences in which it lives and moves. Thus it is clearly evident that success attracts more success, and failure attracts more failure—a truth that has long been known to men, although but few have understood the reason for this strange phenomenon.

It is known that the person who has been a failure may become a most outstanding success by close association with those who think and act in terms of success, but not every one knows that this is true because the law of Cosmic Habitforce transmits the "success consciousness" from the mind of the successful man to the mind of the unsuccessful one who is closely related to him in the daily affairs of life.

Whenever any two minds contact each other there is born of that contact a third mind patterned after *the stronger* of the two. Most successful men recognize this truth and frankly admit that their success began with their close association with some person whose positive mental attitude they either consciously or unconsciously appropriated.

Cosmic Habitforce is silent, unseen and unperceived through any of the five physical senses. That is why it has not been more widely recognized, for most men do not attempt to understand the intangible forces of Nature, nor do they interest themselves in abstract principles. However, these intangibles and abstractions represent the real powers of the universe, and they are the real basis of everything that is tangible and concrete, the source from which tangibility and concreteness are derived.

Understand the working principle of Cosmic Habitforce and you will have no difficulty in interpreting Emerson's essay on Compensation, for he was rubbing elbows with the law of Cosmic Habitforce when he wrote this famous essay.

And Sir Isaac Newton likewise came near to the complete recognition of this law when he made his discovery of the law of gravitation. Had he gone but a brief distance beyond where his discovery ended he might have helped to reveal the same law which holds our little earth in space and relates it systematically to all other planets in both Time and Space; the same law that relates human beings to each other and relates every individual to himself through his *thought habits*.

The term "Habitforce" is self-explanatory. It is a force which works through established habits. And every living thing below the intelligence of man lives, reproduces itself and fulfills its earthly mission in direct response to the power of Cosmic Habitforce through what we call "instinct."

Man alone has been given the privilege of choice in connection with his living habits, and these he may fix by the patterns of his thoughts—the one and only privilege over which any individual has been given complete right of control.

Man may think in terms of self-imposed limitations of fear and doubt and envy and greed and poverty, and Cosmic Habitforce will translate these thoughts into their material equivalent. Or he may think in terms of opulence and plenty, and this same law will translate his thoughts into their physical counterpart.

In this manner may one control his earthly destiny to an astounding degree—simply by exercising his privilege of shaping his own thoughts. But once these thoughts have been shaped into definite patterns they are taken over by the law of Cosmic Habitforce and are made into permanent habits, and they remain as such unless and until they have been supplanted by *different and stronger* thought patterns.

Now we come to the consideration of one of the most profound of all truths; the fact that most men who attain the higher brackets of success seldom do so until they have undergone some tragedy or emergency which reached deeply into their souls and reduced them to that circumstance of life which men call "failure."

The reason for this strange phenomenon is readily recognized by those who understand the law of Cosmic Habitforce, for it consists in the fact that these disasters and tragedies of life serve to break up the established habits of man—habits which have led him eventually to the inevitable results of failure—and thus break the grip of Cosmic Habitforce and allow him to formulate new and better habits.

The War Within The Self

Wars grow out of maladjustments in the relationships of men! These maladjustments are the results of the negative thoughts of men which have grown until they assume *mass proportions*. The spirit of any nation is but the sum total of the dominating thought-habits of its people.

And the same is true of individuals, for here too the spirit of the individual is determined by his dominating thought habits. Most individuals are at war, in one way or another, throughout their lives. They are at war with their own conflicting thoughts and emotions. They are at war in their family relationships and in their occupational and social relationships.

Recognize this truth and you will understand the real power and the benefits which are available to those who live by the Golden Rule, for this great rule *will save you from the conflicts of personal warfare*.

Recognize it and you will understand also the real purpose and benefits of a Definite Major Purpose, for once that purpose has been fixed in the consciousness, by one's thought habits, it will be taken over by Cosmic Habitforce and carried out to its logical conclusion, *by whatever practical means that may be available*.

Cosmic Habitforce does not suggest to an individual what he shall desire, or whether his thought habits shall be positive or negative, but it does act upon all his thought habits by crystallizing them into varying degrees of permanency and translating them into their physical equivalent, through inspired motivation to action.

It not only fixes the thought-habits of individuals, but it fixes also the thought-habits of groups and masses of people, according to the pattern established by the preponderance of their individual dominating thoughts.

The same rule applies to the individual who thinks and talks of disease. At first he is regarded as a hypochondriac— one who suffers with imaginary illness—but when the habit is maintained the disease thus manifested, or one very closely akin to it, generally makes its appearance. Cosmic Habitforce attends to this! For it is true that any thought held in the mind through repetition begins immediately to translate itself into its physical equivalent, by every practical means that may be available.

It is a sad commentary on the intelligence of people to observe that more than three-fourths of the people who have the full benefits of a great country such as ours, should go all the way through life in poverty and want, but the reason for this is not difficult to understand if one recognizes the working principle of Cosmic Habitforce.

Poverty is the direct result of a "poverty consciousness" which results from thinking in terms of poverty, fearing poverty, and talking of poverty.

131

If you desire opulence, give orders to your subconscious mind to produce opulence, thus developing a "prosperity consciousness," and see how quickly your economic condition will improve.

First comes the "consciousness" of that which you desire; then follows the physical or mental manifestation of your desires. The "consciousness" is your responsibility. It is something you must create by your daily thoughts, or by meditation if you prefer to make known your desires in that manner. In this manner one may ally himself with no less a power than that of the Creator of all things.

"I have come to the conclusion," said a great philosopher, "that the acceptance of poverty, or the acceptance of ill health, is an open confession of the lack of Faith."

We do a lot of proclaiming of Faith, but our actions belie our words. Faith is a state of mind that may become permanent only by actions. Belief alone is not sufficient, for as the great philosopher has said, "Faith without works is dead."

The law of Cosmic Habitforce is Nature's own creation. It is the one universal principle through which order and system and harmony are carried out in the entire operation of the universe, from the largest star that hangs in the heavens to the smallest atoms of matter.

It is a power that is equally available to the weak and the strong, the rich and the poor, the sick and the well. It provides the solution to all human problems.

The major purpose of the seventeen principles of this philosophy is that of aiding the individual to adapt himself to the power of Cosmic Habitforce by self-discipline in connection with the formation of his habits of thought.

17 Elements of the Master-Key

Let us turn now to a brief review of these principles, so that we may understand their relationship to Cosmic Habitforce. Let us observe how these principles are so related that they blend together and form the Master-Key which unlocks the doors to the solution of all problems.

The analysis begins with the first principle of the philosophy:

(a) THE HABIT OF GOING THE EXTRA MILE.

This principle is given first position because it aids in conditioning the mind for the rendering of useful service. And this conditioning prepares the way for the second principle—

(b) DEFINITENESS OF PURPOSE.

With the aid of this principle one may give organized direction to the principle of Going The Extra Mile, and make sure that it leads in the direction of his major purpose and becomes cumulative in its effects. These two principles alone will take anyone very far up the ladder of achievement, but those who are aiming for the higher goals of life will need much help on the way, and this help is available through the application of the third principle—

(c) THE MASTER MIND.

Through the application of this principle one begins to experience a new and a greater sense of power which is not available to the individual mind, as it bridges one's personal deficiencies and provides him, when necessary, with any portion of *the combined knowledge of mankind* which has been accumulated down through the ages. But this sense of power will not be complete until one acquires the art of receiving guidance through the fourth principle—

(d) APPLIED FAITH.

Here the individual begins to tune in on the powers of Infinite Intelligence, which is a benefit that is available only to the person who has conditioned his mind to receive it. Here the individual begins to take full possession of his own mind by mastering all fears, worries and doubts, by recognizing his oneness with the source of all power.

These four principles have been rightly called the "Big Four" because they are capable of providing more power than the average man needs to carry him to great heights of personal achievement. But they are adequate only for the very few who have other needed qualities of success, such as those which are provided by the fifth principle.

(e) PLEASING PERSONALITY.

A pleasing personality enables a man to sell himself and his ideas to other men. Hence it is an essential for all who desire to become the guiding influence in a Master Mind alliance. But observe carefully how definitely the four preceding principles tend to give one a pleasing personality. These five principles are capable of providing one with stupendous personal power, but not enough power to insure him against defeat, for defeat is a circumstance that every man meets many times throughout his lifetime; hence the necessity of understanding and applying the sixth principle—

(f) HABIT OF LEARNING FROM DEFEAT.

Notice that this principle begins with the word "habit," which means that it must be accepted and applied as a matter of habit, under all the circumstances of defeat. In this principle may be found hope sufficient to inspire a man to make a fresh start when his plans go astray, as go astray they must at one time or another.

Observe how greatly the source of personal power has increased through the application of these six principles. The individual has found out where he is going in life; he has acquired the friendly cooperation of all whose services are needed to help him reach his goal; he has made himself pleasing, thereby insuring for himself the continued cooperation of others; he has acquired the art of drawing upon the source of Infinite Intelligence and of expressing that power through applied faith; and he has learned to make stepping stones of the stumbling blocks of personal defeat. Despite all of these advantages, however, the man whose Definite Major Purpose leads in the direction of the higher brackets of personal achievement will come many times to the point in his career when he will need the benefits of the seventh principle—

(g) CREATIVE VISION.

This principle enables one to look into the future and to judge it by a comparison with the past, and to build new and better plans for attaining his hopes and aims through the workshop of his imagination. And here, for the first time perhaps, a man may discover his sixth sense and begin to draw upon it for the knowledge which is not available through the organized sources of human experience and accumulated knowledge. But, in order to make sure that he puts this benefit to practical use he must embrace and apply the eighth principle—

(h) PERSONAL INITIATIVE.

This is the principle that starts action and keeps it moving toward definite ends. It insures one against the destructive habits of procrastination, indifference and laziness. An approximation of the importance of this principle may be had by recognizing that it is the "habit-producer" in connection with

134

the seven preceding principles, for it is obvious that the application of no principle may become a *habit* except by the application of personal initiative. The importance of this principle may be further evaluated by recognition of the fact that it is the sole means by which a man may exercise full and complete control over the only thing that the Creator has given him to control, *the power of his own thoughts*.

Thoughts do not organize and direct themselves. They need guidance, inspiration and aid which can be given only by one's personal initiative.

But personal initiative is sometimes misdirected. Therefore it needs the supplemental guidance that is available through the ninth principle—

(i) ACCURATE THINKING.

Accurate thinking not only insures one against the misdirection of personal initiative, but it also insures one against errors of judgment, guess-work and premature decisions. It also protects one against the influence of his own *undependable emotions* by modifying them through the power of reason commonly known as the "head."

Here the individual who has mastered these nine principles will find himself in possession of tremendous power, but personal power may be, and often it is, a dangerous power if it is not controlled and directed through the application of the tenth principle—

(j) SELF-DISCIPLINE.

Self-discipline cannot be had for the mere asking, nor can it be acquired quickly. It is the product of carefully established and carefully maintained habits which in many instances can be acquired only by many years of painstaking effort. So we have come to the point at which the power of the will must be brought into action, *for self-discipline is solely a product of the will*.

Numberless men have risen to great power by the application of the preceding nine principles, only to meet with disaster, or they carry others to defeat by their lack of self-discipline in the use of their power.

This principle, when mastered and applied, gives one complete control over his greatest enemy, himself!

Self-discipline must begin with the application of the eleventh principle—

(k) CONCENTRATION OF ENDEAVOR.

135

The power of concentration is also a product of the will. It is so closely related to self-discipline that the two have been called the "twin-brothers" of this philosophy. Concentration saves one from the dissipation of his energies, and aids him in keeping his mind focused upon the object of his Definite Major Purpose until it has been taken over by the sub-conscious section of the mind and there made ready for translation into its physical equivalent, through the law of Cosmic Habitforce. It is the camera's eye of the imagination through which the detailed outline of one's aims and purposes are recorded in the sub-conscious section of the mind; hence it is indispensable.

Now look again, and see how greatly one's personal power has grown by the application of these eleven principles. But even these are not sufficient for every circumstance of life, for there are times when one must have the friendly co-operation of many people, such as customers in business, or clients in a profession, or votes in an election to public office, all of which may be had through the application of the twelfth principle—

(l) CO-OPERATION.

Co-operation differs from the Master Mind principle in that it is a human relationship that is needed, and may be had, without a definite alliance with others, based upon a complete fusion of the minds for the attainment of a definite purpose.

Without the co-operation of others one cannot attain success in the higher brackets of personal achievement, for co-operation is the means of major value by which one may extend the space he occupies in the minds of others, which is sometimes known as "good-will". Friendly co-operation brings the merchant's customers back as repeat purchasers of his wares, and insures a continuance of patronage from the clients of the professional man. Hence it is a principle that belongs definitely in the philosophy of successful men, regardless of the occupation they may follow.

Co-operation is attained more freely and willingly by the application of the thirteenth principle—

(m) ENTHUSIASM.

Enthusiasm is a contagious state of mind which not only aids one in gaining the co-operation of others, but more important than this, it inspires the individual to draw upon and use the power of his own imagination. It inspires action also

136

in the expression of personal initiative, and leads to the habit of concentration of endeavor. Moreover, it is one of the qualities of major importance of a pleasing personality, and it makes easy the application of the principle of Going The Extra Mile. In addition to all these benefits, enthusiasm gives force and conviction to the spoken word.

Enthusiasm is the product of *motive*, but it is difficult of maintenance without the aid of the fourteenth principle—

(n) THE HABIT OF HEALTH.

Sound physical health provides a suitable housing place for the operation of the mind; hence it is an essential for enduring success, assuming that the word "success" shall embrace all of the requirements for happiness.

Here again the word "habit" comes into prominence, for sound health begins with a "health consciousness" that can be developed only by the right habits of living, sustained through self-discipline.

Sound health provides the basis for enthusiasm, and enthusiasm encourages sound health; so the two are like the hen and the egg; no one can determine which came into existence first, but everyone knows that both are essential for the production of either. Health and enthusiasm are like that. Both are essential for human progress and happiness.

Now take inventory again and count up the gains in power which the individual has attained by the application of these fourteen principles. It has reached proportions so stupendous that it staggers the imagination. Yet it is not sufficient to insure one against failure; therefore we shall have to add the fifteenth principle—

(o) BUDGETING TIME AND MONEY.

Oh! what a headache one gets at the mention of saving of time and the conservation of money. Nearly everyone wishes to spend both time and money freely, but budget and conserve them, never! However, independence and freedom of body and mind, the two great desires of all mankind, cannot become enduring realities without the self-discipline of a strict budgeting system. Hence this principle is of necessity an important essential of the philosophy of individual achievement.

Now we are reaching the ultimate in the attainment of personal power. We have learned the sources of power and how we may tap them and apply them at will to any desired end; and that power is so great that nothing can resist it save only the fact that the individual may unwisely apply it to his own destruction and the destruction of others. Hence, to guide one in the right use of power it is necessary to add the sixteenth principle—

(p) THE GOLDEN RULE *APPLIED*.

Observe the emphasis on the word "applied." Belief in the soundness of the Golden Rule is not enough. To be of enduring benefit, and in order that it may serve as a safe guide in the use of personal power, it must be applied as a matter of habit, in all human relationships.

Quite an order, this! But the benefits which are available through the application of this profound rule of human relationship are worthy of the efforts necessary to develop it into a habit. The penalties for failure to live by this rule are too numerous for description in detail.

Now we have attained the ultimate in personal power, and we have provided ourselves with the necessary insurance against its misuse. What we need from here on out is the means by which this power may be made permanent during our entire lifetime. We shall climax this philosophy, therefore, with the only known principle by which we may attain this desired end—the seventeenth and last principle of this philosophy—

(q) COSMIC HABITFORCE.

Cosmic Habitforce is the principle by which all habits are fixed and made permanent in varying degrees. As stated, it is the controlling principle of this entire philosophy, into which the preceding sixteen principles blend and become a part. And it is the controlling principle of all natural laws of the universe. It is the principle that gives the *fixation of habit* in the application of the preceding principles of this philosophy. Thus it is the controlling factor in conditioning the individual mind for the development and the expression of the "prosperity consciousness" which is so essential in the attainment of personal success.

Mere understanding of the sixteen preceding principles will not lead anyone to the attainment of personal power. The principles must be understood and applied as a matter of strict habit, and habit is the sole work of the law of Cosmic Habitforce.

Cosmic Habitforce is synonymous with the great River of Life to which frequent references have been made previously, for it consists of a negative and a positive potentiality, as do all forms of energy.

The negative application is called "hypnotic rhythm" because it has a hypnotic effect on everything that it contacts. We may see its effects, in one way or another, on every human being.

It is the sole means by which the "poverty consciousness" becomes fixed as a *habit!*

It is the builder of all established *habits* of fear, and envy, and greed, and revenge, and of desire for something for nothing.

It fixes the *habits* of hopelessness and indifference.

And it is the builder of the *habit* of hypochondria, through which millions of people suffer all through their lives with imaginary illness.

It is also the builder of the "failure consciousness" which undermines the self-confidence of millions of people.

In brief, it fixes *all negative habits*, regardless of their nature or effects. Thus it is the "failure" side of the great River of Life.

The "success" side of the River—the positive side—fixes all constructive habits, such as the habit of Definiteness of Purpose, the habit of Going The Extra Mile, the habit of applying the Golden Rule in human relationships, and all the other habits which one must develop and apply in order to get the benefits of the sixteen preceding principles of this philosophy.

Enforcement of Habits

Now let us examine this word "habit"!

Webster's dictionary gives the word many definitions, among them: "Habit implies a settled disposition or tendency *due to repetition*; custom suggests the fact of repetition rather than the tendency to repeat; usage (applying only to a considerable body of people) adds the implication of long acceptation or standing; both custom and usage often suggest authority; as, we do many things mechanically from force of habit."

Webster's definition runs on into considerable additional

139

detail, but no part of it comes within sight of describing the law that fixes all habits; this omission being due no doubt to the fact that the law of Cosmic Habitforce had not been revealed to the editors of this dictionary. But we observe one significant and important word in the Webster definition—the word "repetition." It is important because it describes the means by which any habit is begun.

The habit of Definiteness of Purpose, for example, becomes a habit only by repetition of the thought of that purpose, by bringing the thought into the mind repeatedly; by *repeatedly* submitting the thought to the imagination with a burning desire for its fulfillment, until the imagination creates a practical plan for attaining this desire; by applying the *habit* of Faith in connection with the desire, and doing it so intensely and repeatedly that one may see himself already in possession of the object of his desires, *even before he begins to attain it.*

The building of voluntary positive habits calls for the application of self-discipline, persistence, will-power and Faith, all of which are available to the person who has assimilated the sixteen preceding principles of this philosophy.

Voluntary habit-building is self-discipline in its highest and noblest form of application!

And all voluntary positive habits are the products of will-power directed toward the attainment of definite ends. *They originate with the individual,* not with Cosmic Habitforce. And they must be grounded in the mind through repetition of thoughts and deeds until they are taken over by Cosmic Habitforce and are given fixation, after which they operate automatically.

The word *habit* is an important word in connection with this philosophy of individual achievement, for it represents the real cause of every man's economic, social, professional, occupational and spiritual condition in life. We are where we are and what we are because of our fixed habits. And we may be where we wish to be and what we wish to be only by the development and the maintenance of our *voluntary habits.*

Thus we see that this entire philosophy leads inevitably to an understanding and application of the law of Cosmic Habitforce—the power of fixation of all habits!

The major purpose of each of the sixteen preceding principles of this philosophy is that of aiding the individual in the development of a particular, specialized form of habit that is necessary as a means of enabling him to *take full possession of his own mind!* This too must become a habit!

Mind-power is always actively engaged on one side of the River of Life or the other. The purpose of this philosophy is to enable one to develop and maintain habits of thought and of deed which keep his mind concentrated upon the "success" side of the River. This is the sole burden of the philosophy.

Mastery and assimilation of the philosophy, like every other desirable thing, has a definite price which must be paid before its benefits may be enjoyed. That price, among other things, is eternal vigilance, determination, persistence and the will to make Life pay off on one's own terms instead of accepting substitutes of poverty and misery and disillusionment.

There are two ways of relating one's self to Life.

One is that of playing horse while Life rides. The other is that of becoming the rider while Life plays horse. The choice as to whether one becomes the horse or the rider is the privilege of every person, but this much is certain: if one does not choose to become the rider of Life, he is sure to be forced to become the horse. Life either rides or is ridden. It never stands still.

The "Ego" and Cosmic Habitforce

As a student of this philosophy you are interested in the method by which one may transmute the power of thought into its physical equivalent. And you are interested in learning how to relate yourself to others in a spirit of harmony.

Unfortunately our public schools have been silent on both of these important needs. "Our educational system," said Dr. Henry C. Link, "has concentrated on mental development and has failed to give any understanding of the way emotional and personality habits are acquired or corrected."

His indictment is not without a sound foundation. The public school system has failed in the obligation of which Dr. Link complains, because the law of Cosmic Habitforce was but recently revealed, and even now it has not been recognized by the great mass of educators.

Everyone knows that practically everything we do, from

141

the time we begin to walk, is the result of habit. Walking and talking are habits. Our manner of eating and drinking is a habit. Our sex activities are the result of habit. Our relationships with others, whether they are positive or negative, are the results of habits, but few people understand why or how we form habits.

Habits are inseparably related to the human ego. Therefore, let us turn to the analysis of this greatly misunderstood subject of the ego. But first let us recognize that the ego is the medium through which faith and all other states of mind operate.

Throughout this philosophy great emphasis has been placed upon the distinction between passive faith and active faith. The ego is the medium of expression of all action. Therefore we must know something of its nature and possibilities in order that we may make the best use of it. We must learn how to stimulate the ego to action and how to control and guide it to the attainment of definite ends.

Above all, we must disabuse our minds of the popular error of believing the ego to be only a medium for expression of vanity. The word "ego" is of Latin origin, and it means "I". But it also connotes a driving force which may be organized and made to serve as the medium for translating desire into faith, through action.

The Misunderstood Power of the Ego

The word ego has reference to all the factors of one's personality!

Therefore it is obvious that the ego is subject to development, guidance and control through voluntary habits—habits which we deliberately and with purpose aforethought develop.

A great philosopher who devoted his entire life to the study of the human body and the mind, provided us with a practical foundation for the study of the ego when he stated:

"Your body, whether living or dead, is a collection of millions of little energies that can never die.

"These energies are separate and individual; at times they act in some degree of harmony.

"The human body is a drifting mechanism of life, capable but not accustomed to control the forces within, except as

142

habit, will, cultivation or special excitement (through the emotion) may marshal these forces to the accomplishment of some important end.

"We are satisfied from many experiments that this power of marshalling and using these energies can be, in every person, cultivated to a high degree.

"The air, sunlight, food and water you take, are agents of a force which comes from the sky and earth. You idly float upon the tide of circumstances to make up your day's life, and the opportunities of being something better than you are drift beyond your reach and pass away.

"Humanity is hemmed in by so many influences that, from time immemorial, no real effort has been made to gain control of the impulses that run loose in the world. It has been, and still is, easier to let things go as they will rather than exert the will to direct them.

"But the dividing line between success and failure is found at the stage where aimless drifting ceases. (Where Definiteness of Purpose begins.)

"We are all creatures of emotions, passions, circumstances and accident. What the mind will be, what the heart will be, what the body will be, are problems which are shaped to the drift of life, even when special attention is given to any of them.

"If you will sit down and think for a while, *you will be surprised to know how much of your life has been mere drift.*

"Look at any created life, and see its efforts to express itself. The tree sends its branches toward the sunlight, struggles through its leaves to inhale air; and even underground sends forth its roots in search of water and the minerals it needs for food. This you call inanimate life; but it represents a force that comes from some source and operates for some purpose.

"There is no place on the globe where energy is not found.

"The air is so loaded with it that in the cold north the sky shines in boreal rays; and wherever the frigid temperature yields to the warmth, the electric conditions may alarm man. Water is but a liquid union of gases, and is charged with electrical, mechanical and chemical energies, any one of which is capable of doing great service and great damage to man.

"Even ice, in its coldest phase, has energy, for it is not subdued, nor even still; its force has broken mountain rocks into fragments. This energy about us we are drinking in water, eating in food and breathing in air. Not a chemical molecule is free from it; not an atom can exist without it. We are a combination of individual energies."

Man consists of two forces, one tangible, in the form of his physical body, with its myriad individual cells numbering billions, each of which is endowed with intelligence and energy; and the other intangible, in the form of an ego—the organized dictator of the body which may control man's thoughts and deeds.

Science teaches us the tangible portion of a man weighing one hundred and sixty pounds is composed of about seventeen chemical elements, all of which are known. They are:

> 95 pounds of oxygen.
> 38 pounds of carbon.
> 15 pounds of hydrogen.
> 4 pounds of nitrogen.
> $4^{1}/_{2}$ pounds of calcium.
> 6 ounces of chlorine.
> 4 ounces of sulphur.
> $3^{1}/_{2}$ ounces of potassium.
> 3 ounces of sodium.
> $^{1}/_{4}$ ounce of iron.
> $2^{1}/_{2}$ ounces of fluorine.
> 2 ounces of magnesium.
> $1^{1}/_{2}$ ounces of silicon.

Small traces of arsenic, iodine and aluminum.

These tangible parts of man are worth only a few cents commercially and may be purchased in any modern chemical plant.

Add to these chemical elements a well developed and properly organized and controlled ego, and they may be worth any price the owner sets upon them. The ego is a power which cannot be purchased at any price, but it can be developed and shaped to fit any desired pattern. The development takes place through organized habits which are made permanent by the law of Cosmic Habitforce, which carries out the thought-patterns one develops through controlled thought.

One of the major differences between men who make valuable contributions to mankind and those who merely take up space in the world, is mainly a difference in egos, be-

The Law of Cosmic Habitforce ◾

cause the ego is the driving force behind all forms of human action.

Liberty and freedom of body and mind—the two major desires of all people—are available in exact proportion to the development and use one makes of the ego. Every person who has properly related himself to his own ego has both liberty and freedom in whatever proportions he desires.

A man's ego determines the manner in which he relates himself to all other people. More important than this, it determines the policy under which a man relates his own body and mind, wherein is patterned every hope, aim and purpose by which he fixes his destiny in life.

A man's ego is his greatest asset or his greatest liability, according to the way he relates himself to it. The ego is the sum total of one's thought habits which have been fastened upon him through the automatic operation of the law of Cosmic Habitforce.

Every highly successful person possesses a well-developed and highly disciplined ego, but there is a third factor associated with the ego which determines its potency for good or evil—the self-control necessary to enable one to transmute its power into any desired purpose.

"Training" the Ego

The starting point of all individual achievements is some plan by which one's ego can be inspired with a "success consciousness". The person who succeeds must do so by properly developing his own ego, impressing it with the object of his desires, and removing from it all forms of limitation, fear and doubt which lead to the dissipation of the power of the ego.

Auto-suggestion (or self-hypnosis) is the medium by which one may attune his ego to any desired rate of vibration and charge it with the attainment of any desired purpose.

Unless you catch the full significance of the principle of auto-suggestion you will miss the most important part of this analysis, because the power of the ego is fixed entirely by the application of self-suggestion.

When this self-suggestion attains the status of faith the ego becomes limitless in its power.

145

The ego is kept alive and active, and it is given power by constant feeding. Like the physical body, the ego cannot and will not subsist without food.

It must be fed with Definiteness of Purpose.

It must be fed with Personal Initiative.

It must be fed with Continuous Action, through well organized plans.

It must be supported with Enthusiasm.

It must be fed by Controlled Attention, directed to a definite end.

It must be controlled and directed through Self-discipline.

And it must be supported with Accurate Thought.

No man can become the master of anything or anyone until he becomes the master of his own ego.

No man can express himself in terms of opulence while most of his thought-power is given over to the maintenance of a "poverty consciousness." Nevertheless, one should not lose sight of the fact that many men of great wealth began in poverty—a fact which suggests that this and all other fears can be conquered and removed from interference with the ego.

In the one word, ego, may be found the composite effects of all the principles of individual achievement described in this philosophy, co-ordinated into one single unit of power which may be directed to any desired end by any individual who is the complete master of his ego.

We are preparing you to accept the fact that the most important power which is available to you—the one power which will determine whether you succeed or fail in your life's ambition—is that which is represented by your own ego.

We are also preparing you to brush aside that time-worn belief which associates the ego with self-love, vanity and vulgarity, and to recognize the truth that the ego is all there is of a man outside of the few cents' worth of chemicals, of which his physical body is composed.

Sex is the great creative force of man. It is definitely associated with and is an important part of one's ego. Both sex and the ego got their bad reputations from the fact that both are subject to destructive as well as constructive application, and both have been abused by the ignorant, from the beginning of the history of mankind.

The egoist who makes himself offensive through the expression of his ego is one who has not discovered how to relate himself to his ego in a manner which gives it constructive use.

Constructive application of the ego is made through the expressions of one's hopes, desires, aims, ambitions and plans, and not by boastfulness or self-love. The motto of the person who has his ego under control is, "Deeds, not words."

The desire to be great, to be recognized and to have personal power, is a healthy desire; but an open expression of one's belief in his own greatness is an indication that he has not taken possession of his ego, that he has allowed it to take possession of him; and you may be sure that his proclamations of greatness are but a cloak with which to shield some fear or inferiority complex.

The Ego and Mental Attitude

Understand the real nature of your ego and you will understand the real significance of the Master Mind principle. Moreover, you will recognize that to be of the greatest service to you, the members of your Master Mind alliance must be in complete sympathy with your hopes, aims and purposes; that they must not be in competition with you in any manner whatsoever. They must be willing to subordinate their own desires and personalities entirely for the attainment of your major purpose in life.

They must have confidence in you and your integrity, and they must respect you. They must be willing to accentuate your virtues and make allowances for your faults. They must be willing to permit you to be yourself and live your own life in your own way at all times. Lastly, they must receive from you some form of benefit which will make you as beneficial to them as they are to you.

Failure to observe the last mentioned requirement will bring an end to the power of your Master Mind alliance.

Men relate themselves to one another in whatever capacities they may be associated because of a motive or motives. There can be no permanent human relationship based upon an indefinite or vague motive, or upon no motive at all. Failure to recognize this truth has cost many men the difference between penury and opulence.

The power which takes over the ego and clothes it with the material counterparts of the thoughts which give it shape, is the law of Cosmic Habitforce. This law does not give quality or quantity to the ego; it merely takes what it finds and translates it into its physical equivalent.

The men of great achievement are, and they have always been, those who deliberately feed, shape and control their own egos, leaving no part of the task to luck or chance, or to the varying vicissitudes of life.

Every person may control the shaping of his own ego, but from that point on he has no more to do with what happens than does the farmer have anything to do with what happens to the seed he sows in the soil of the earth. The inexorable law of Cosmic Habitforce causes every living thing to perpetuate itself after its kind, and it translates the picture which a man paints of his ego into its physical equivalent, as definitely as it develops an acorn into an oak tree, and no outside aid whatsoever is required, except time.

From these statements it is obvious that we are not only advocating the deliberate development and control of the ego, but also we are definitely warning that no man can hope to succeed in any calling without such control over his ego.

So that there may be no misunderstanding as to what is meant by the term "a properly developed ego" we shall describe briefly the factors which enter into its development, viz:

First, one must ally himself with one or more persons who will co-ordinate their minds with his in a spirit of perfect harmony for the attainment of a definite purpose, and that alliance must be continuous and active.

Moreover, the alliance must consist of people whose spiritual and mental qualities, education, sex and age are suited for aiding in the attainment of the purpose of the alliance. For example, Andrew Carnegie's Master Mind alliance was made up of more than twenty men, each of whom brought to the alliance some quality of mind, experience, education or knowledge which was directly related to the object of the alliance and not available through any of the other members of the alliance.

Second, having placed himself under the influence of

the proper associates, one must adopt some definite plan by which to attain the object of the alliance and proceed to put that plan into action. The plan may be a composite plan created by the joint efforts of all the members of the Master Mind group.

If one plan proves to be unsound or inadequate, it must be supplemented or supplanted by others, until a plan is found which will work. But there must be no change in the purpose of the alliance.

Third, one must remove himself from the range of influence of every person and every circumstance which has even a slight tendency to cause him to feel inferior or incapable of attaining the object of his purpose. Positive egos do not grow in negative environments. On this point there can be no excuse for a compromise, and failure to observe it will prove fatal to the chances of success.

The line must be so clearly drawn between a man and those who exercise any form of negative influence over him that he closes the door tightly against every such person, no matter what previous ties of friendship or obligation or blood relationship may have existed between them.

Fourth, one must close the door tightly against every thought of any past experience or circumstance which tends to make him feel inferior or unhappy. Strong, vital egos cannot be developed by dwelling on thoughts of past unpleasant experiences. Vital egos thrive on the hopes and desires of the yet unattained objectives.

Thoughts are the building-blocks from which the human ego is constructed. Cosmic Habitforce is the cement which binds these blocks together in permanency, through fixed habits. When the job is finished it represents, right down to the smallest detail, the nature of the thoughts which went into the building.

Fifth, one must surround himself with every possible physical means of impressing his mind with the nature and the purpose of the ego he is developing. For example, the author should set up his workshop in a room decorated with pictures and the works of authors in his field whom he most admires. He should fill his book shelves with books related to his own work. He should surround himself with every possible means of conveying to his ego the exact picture of himself which he expects to express, because that picture is the pattern which

149

the law of Cosmic Habitforce will pick up; the picture which it translates into its physical equivalent.

Sixth, the properly developed ego is at all times under the control of the individual. There must be no over-inflation of the ego in the direction of "egomania" by which some men destroy themselves.

Egomania reveals itself by a mad desire to control others by force. Striking examples of such men are Adolph Hitler, Benito Mussolini and the Kaiser.

In the development of the ego, one's motto might well be, "Not too much, not too little, of anything." When men begin to thirst for control over others, or begin to accumulate large sums of money which they cannot or do not use constructively, they are treading upon dangerous grounds. Power of this nature grows of its own accord and soon gets out of control.

Nature has provided man with a safety-valve through which she deflates the ego and relieves the pressure of its influence when an individual goes beyond certain limits in the development of the ego. Emerson called it the law of Compensation, but whatever it is, it operates with inexorable definiteness.

Napoleon Bonaparte began to die, because of his crushed ego, on the day he landed on St. Helena Island.

People who quit work and retire from all forms of activity, after having led active lives, generally atrophy and die soon thereafter. If they live they are usually miserable and unhappy. A healthy ego is one which is always in use and under complete control.

Seventh, the ego is constantly undergoing changes, for better or for worse, because of the nature of one's thought habits. The two factors which force these changes upon one are Time and the law of Cosmic Habitforce.

Time for Growth

Here I desire to bring to your attention the importance of Time as a significant factor in the operation of Cosmic Habitforce. Just as seeds which are planted in the soil of the earth require definite periods of Time for their germination, development and growth, so do ideas, impulses of thought

150

and desires which are planted in the mind require definite periods of Time during which the law of Cosmic Habitforce gives them life and action.

There is no adequate means of describing or pre-determining the exact period of Time which is required for the transformation of a desire into its physical equivalent. The nature of the desire, the circumstances which are related to it, and the intensity of the desire, are all determining factors in connection with the Time required for transformation from the thought stage to the physical stage.

The state of mind known as faith is so favorable for the quick change of desire into its physical equivalent that it has been known to make the change almost instantaneously.

Man matures physically in about twenty years, but mentally—which means the ego—he requires from thirty-five to sixty years for maturity. This fact explains why men seldom begin to accumulate material riches in great abundance, or to attain outstanding records of achievement in other directions, until they are about fifty years of age.

The ego which can inspire a man to acquire and retain great material wealth is of necessity one which has undergone self-discipline, through which he acquires self-confidence, definiteness of purpose, personal initiative, imagination, accuracy of judgment and other qualities, without which no ego has the power to procure and hold wealth in abundance.

These qualities come through the proper *use* of Time. Observe that we did not say they come through the lapse of Time. Through the operation of Cosmic Habitforce every individual's thought habits, whether they are negative or positive, whether of opulence or of poverty, are woven into the pattern of his ego, and there they are given permanent form which determines the nature and the extent of his spiritual and physical status.

The Ego Behind Success

About the beginning of the 1929 economic depression the owner of a small beauty salon turned over a back room in her place of business to an old man who needed a place to sleep.

The man had no money, but he did have considerable knowledge of the methods of compounding cosmetics.

The owner of the salon gave him a place to sleep and provided him with an opportunity to pay for his room by compounding the cosmetics she used in her business.

Soon the two entered into a Master Mind alliance which was destined to bring each of them economic independence. First, they entered into a business partnership, with the object of compounding cosmetics to be sold from house to house; the woman providing the money for the raw materials, the man doing the work.

After a few years the Master Mind arrangement between the two had proved so profitable that they decided to make it permanent by marriage, although there was a difference of more than twenty-five years in their ages.

The man had been in the cosmetic business for the better portion of his adult life, but he had never achieved success. The young woman had barely made a living from her beauty salon. The happy combination of the two brought them into possession of a power which neither had known prior to their alliance, and they began to succeed financially.

At the beginning of the depression they were compounding cosmetics in one small room, and selling their products personally from door to door. By the end of the depression, some eight years later, they were compounding their cosmetics in a large factory which they had bought and paid for, and had more than a hundred employees working steadily, and more than four thousand agents selling their products throughout the nation.

During this period they accumulated a fortune of over two million dollars, despite the fact that they were operating during depression years when such luxuries as cosmetics were naturally hard to sell.

They have placed themselves beyond the need for money for the remainder of their lives. Moreover, they have gained financial freedom on precisely the same knowledge and the same opportunities they possessed prior to their Master Mind alliance, when both were poverty-stricken.

We wish the names of these two interesting people could be revealed, but the circumstances of their alliance and the nature of the analysis we shall now present makes this impractical. Nevertheless, we are free to describe what we con-

152

ceive to be the source of their astounding achievement, viewing every circumstance of their relationship entirely from the viewpoint of an unbiased analyst who is seeking only to present a true picture of the facts.

The motive which brought these two people together in a Master Mind alliance was definitely economic in nature. The woman had previously been married to a man who failed to earn a living for her and who deserted her when her child was an infant. The man also had been previously married.

There was not the slightest indication of the emotion of love as a motive for their marriage. The motive was entirely a mutual desire for economic freedom.

The business and the elaborate home in which the couple live are entirely dominated by the old man, who sincerely believes that he is responsible for both.

Their house is expensively furnished, but no one—not even invited guests—is permitted to take a turn at the piano, or to sit in one of the chairs in the living room, without special invitation from the "lord and master" of the household.

The main dining room is equipped with ornate furniture, including a long dining table which is suitable for use on "state" occasions, but the family is never permitted to use it on other occasions. They dine in the breakfast room, and nothing may be served at the table at any time except food of the "master's" choice.

A gardener is employed to attend the gardens, but no one is permitted to cut a flower without special invitation from the head of the house.

Such conversations as are carried on by the family are conducted entirely by the head of the house, and no one may intervene, not even to ask a question or to offer a remark, unless he invites it. His wife never speaks unless she is definitely requested to do so, and then her speech is very brief and carefully weighed so as not to irritate her "master."

Their business is incorporated and the man is the president of the company. He has an elaborate office which is furnished with a large hand-carved desk and overstuffed chairs.

On the wall, directly in front of his desk, is an enormous oil painting of himself at which he gazes, sometimes for an hour at a time, with obvious approval.

When he speaks of the business, and particularly of the unusual success it enjoyed during the country's worst business depression, the man takes full credit for all that has been accomplished, and he never mentions his wife's name in connection with the business.

While the wife goes to business daily, she has no office and no desk. She is apt to be found strolling around among the workers, or assisting one of the girls in wrapping packages as nonchalantly as if she were an ordinary paid employee.

The man's name is on every package of merchandise which leaves the factory. It is printed in large letters on every delivery truck they operate, and it appears in large type on every piece of sales literature and in every advertisement they publish. The wife's name is conspicuous by its total absence.

The man believes that he built the business; that he operates it; that it could not operate without him. The truth of the matter is precisely the opposite. His ego built the business, runs it, and the business might continue to run as well or better without his presence as with it, for the very good reason that his *wife developed that ego*, and she could have done the same for any other man under similar circumstances.

Patiently, wisely and with purpose aforethought, this man's wife completely submerged her own personality into that of her husband, and step by step she fed his ego the type of food which removed from it every trace of his former inferiority complex, which was born of a lifetime of deprivation and failure. She hypnotized her husband into believing himself to be a great business tycoon.

Whatever degree of ego this man may have possessed before it came under the influence of a clever woman, had died of starvation. She revived his ego, nurtured it, fed it and developed it into a power of stupendous proportions despite his eccentric nature and his lack of business ability.

In truth every business policy, every business move, and every forward step the business has taken was the result of the wife's ideas, which she so cleverly planted in her husband's mind that he failed to recognize their source. In reality she is the brains of the business, he the mere window dressing; *but the combination is unbeatable,* as evidenced by their astounding financial achievements.

The manner in which this woman completely effaced herself was not only convincing evidence of her complete self-control, but it was evidence of her wisdom, for she probably

154

knew she could not have accomplished the same results alone, or by any other methods than those she adopted.

This woman has very little formal education, and we have no idea how or where she learned enough about the operation of the human mind to inspire her to merge her entire personality with that of her husband for the purpose of developing in him the ego he now has. Perhaps the natural intuition which many women possess was responsible for her successful procedure. Whatever it was, she did a thorough job, and it served the ends she sought by bringing her economic security.

Care and Feeding of the Ego

Here then is evidence that the major difference between poverty and riches is merely the difference between an ego that is dominated by an inferiority complex and one that is dominated by a feeling of superiority. This old man might have died a homeless pauper if a clever woman had not blended her mind with his in such a way as to feed his ego with thoughts of, and belief in, his ability to attain opulence.

This is a conclusion from which there is no escape. Moreover, this case is only one of many that could be cited which prove that the human ego must be fed, organized and directed to definite ends if one is to succeed in any walk of life.

The Key is in Your Hands

You now have, in the seventeen principles of this philosophy, all that is required to place you in possession of the Master-Key!

You are now in possession of all the practical knowledge which has been used by successful men from the dawn of civilization to the present.

This is a complete philosophy of life—sufficient for every human need. It holds the secret to the solution of all human problems. And it has been presented in terms which the humblest person may understand.

You may not aspire to become internationally famous, but you can and you should aspire to make yourself useful in order that you may occupy as much space in the world as your ego desires.

Every man comes finally to resemble those who make the strongest impression upon his ego. We are all creatures of imitation, and naturally we endeavor to imitate the heroes of our choice. This is a natural and healthful trait.

Fortunate indeed is the man whose hero is a person of great Faith, because hero-worship carries with it something of the nature of the hero one worships.

In conclusion let us summarize what has been said on the subject of the ego by calling attention to the fact that it represents the fertile garden spot of the mind wherein one may develop all the stimuli which inspire active Faith, or by neglecting to do so he may allow this fertile soil to produce a negative crop of fear and doubt and indecision which will lead to failure.

The amount of space you occupy in the world is now a matter of choice with you. The Master-Key To Riches is in your hands. You stand before the last gate which separates you from the success you desire. The gate will not open to you without your demand that it do so. You must use the Master-Key by making the seventeen principles of this philosophy *your own!*

You now have at your command a *complete philosophy* of life that is sufficient for the solution of every individual problem.

It is a philosophy of principles, some combination of which has been responsible for every individual success in every occupation or calling, although many may have used the philosophy successfully without recognizing the seventeen principles by the names we have given them.

No essential factor of successful achievement has been omitted. The philosophy embraces them all and describes them in words and similes that are well within the understanding of a majority of the people.

It is a philosophy of concreteness that touches only rarely the abstractions, and then only when necessary. It is free from academic terms and phrases which all too often serve only to confuse the average person.

The overall purpose of the philosophy is to enable one to

156

get from where he stands to where he wishes to be, *both economically and spiritually;* thus it prepares one to enjoy the abundant life which the Creator intended all people to enjoy.

And it leads to the attainment of "riches" in the broadest and fullest meaning of the word, *including the twelve most important of all riches.*

The world has been greatly enriched by abstract philosophies, from the days of Plato, Socrates, Copernicus, Aristotle and many others of the same profound caliber of thinkers, on down to the days of Ralph Waldo Emerson and William James.

Now the world has a complete, concrete philosophy of individual achievement that provides the individual with the practical means by which he may take possession of his own mind and direct it to the attainment of peace of mind, harmony in human relationships, economic security, and the fuller life known as happiness.

Not as an apology, but to serve as an explanation, I shall call your attention to the fact that throughout this analysis of the seventeen principles we have emphasized the more important of these principles by continuous reference to them. The repetition was not accidental!

It was deliberate and necessary because of the tendency of all mankind to be unimpressed by new ideas or new interpretations of old truths.

Repetition has been necessary also because of the interrelationship of the seventeen principles, being connected as they are like the links of a chain, each one extending into and becoming a part of the principle preceding it and the principle following it.

And lastly, let us recognize that repetition of ideas is one of the basic principles of effective pedagogy and the central core of all effective advertising. Therefore it is not only justified, but it is definitely necessary as a means of human progress.

When you have assimilated this philosophy you will have a better education than the majority of people who graduate from college with the Master of Arts degree. You will be in possession of all the more useful knowledge which has been organized from the experiences of the most successful men this nation has produced, and you will have it in a form which you can understand and apply.

But remember that the responsibility for the proper use of this knowledge will be yours. The mere possession of the knowledge will avail you nothing. Its *use* is what will count!

Chapter Ten

SELF-DISCIPLINE

The man who acquires the ability to take full possession of his own mind may take possession of everything else to which he is justly entitled.

—Andrew Carnegie.

We shall now reveal the methods by which one may take possession of his own mind.

We begin with a quotation from a man who proved the truth of his statement by his astounding achievements.

Those who knew him best, who worked with him most closely, say that his most outstanding trait of character consisted in the fact that he took full possession of his own mind at an early age, and never gave up any portion of his right to think his own thoughts.

What an achievement! and what a blessing it would be if every man could truthfully say, "I am the master of my fate; I am the Captain of my soul."

The Creator probably intended it to be so!

If it had been intended otherwise man would not have been limited solely to the right of control over but one power—the power of his own thoughts.

We go all the way through life searching for freedom of body and mind, yet most men never find it! Why? The Creator provided the means by which men may be free, and gave every man access to these means; and also inspired every man with impelling motives for the attainment of freedom.

Why then do men go through life imprisoned in a jail of their own making, when the key to the door is so easily within their reach? The jail of poverty, the jail of ill health, the jail of fear, the jail of ignorance.

The desire for freedom of body and mind is a universal desire among all peoples, but few ever attain it because most men who search for it look everywhere except the one and only source from which it may come—*within their own minds.*

The desire for riches is also a universal desire, but most men never come within sight of the real riches of life because they do not recognize that all riches begin within their own minds.

Men search all their lives for power and fame without attaining either, because they do not recognize that the real source of both is within their own minds.

The mechanism of the mind is a profound system of organized power which can be released only by one means, and that is *by strict self-discipline.*

The mind that is properly disciplined and directed to definite ends is an irresistible power that recognizes no such reality as permanent defeat. It organizes defeat and converts it into victory; makes stepping-stones of stumbling-blocks; hitches its wagon to a star and uses the forces of the universe to carry it within easy grasp of its every desire.

And the man who masters himself through self-discipline never can be mastered by others!

Self-discipline is one of the Twelve Riches, but it is much more; it is an important prerequisite for the attainment of all riches, including freedom of body and mind, power and fame, and all the material things that men call wealth.

It is the sole means by which one may focus the mind upon the objective of a Definite Major Purpose until the law of Cosmic Habitforce takes over the pattern of that purpose and begins to translate it into its material equivalent.

It is the key to the *volitional power of the will* and the *emotions of the heart,* for it is the means by which these two may be mastered and balanced, one against the other, and directed to definite ends in *accurate thinking.*

It is the directing force in the maintenance of a Definite Major Purpose.

It is the source of all persistence and the means by which one may develop the habit of carrying through his plans and purposes.

160

It is the power with which all thought habits are patterned and sustained until they are taken over by the law of Cosmic Habitforce and carried out to their logical climax.

It is the means by which one may take *full and complete control of his mind* and direct it to whatever ends he may desire.

It is indispensable in all leadership.

And it is the power through which one may make of his conscience a co-operator and guide instead of a conspirator.

It is the policeman who clears the mind for the expression of Faith, by the mastery of all fears.

It clears the mind for the expression of Imagination and of Creative Vision.

It does away with indecision and doubt.

It helps one to create and to sustain the "prosperity consciousness" that is essential for the accumulation of material riches, and the "health consciousness" necessary for the maintenance of sound physical health.

Also it operates entirely through the functioning system of the mind. Therefore, let us examine this system so that we may understand the factors of which it consists.

The Ten Factors of the "Mechanism" of Thought

The mind operates through ten factors, some of which operate automatically, while others must be directed through voluntary effort. *Self-discipline is the sole means of this direction.*

These ten factors are:

1. INFINITE INTELLIGENCE: The source of all power of thought, which operates automatically, but it may be organized and directed to definite ends through Definiteness of Purpose.

Infinite Intelligence may be likened to a great reservoir of water that overflows continuously, its branches flowing in small streams in many directions, and giving life to all vegetation and all living things. That portion of the stream which gives life to man supplies him also with the power of thought.

The brain of man may be likened to the water spigot, while the water flowing through the spigot represents Infinite Intelligence. The brain does not generate the power of thought; *it*

161

merely receives that power from Infinite Intelligence and applies it to whatever ends the individual desires.

And remember, this privilege of the control and the direction of thought is the only prerogative over which an individual has been given complete control. He may use it to build, or he may use it to destroy. He may give it direction, through Definiteness of Purpose, or he may neglect to do so, as he chooses.

The exercise of this great privilege is attained solely by self-discipline.

2. THE CONSCIOUS MIND: The individual mind functions through two departments. One is known as the conscious section of the mind; the other as the sub-conscious section. It is the opinion of psychologists that these two sections are comparable to an iceberg, the visible portion above the water line representing the conscious section, the invisible portion below the water line representing the sub-conscious section. Therefore it is obvious that the conscious section of the mind—that portion with which we consciously and voluntarily turn on the power of thought—is but a small portion of the whole, consisting of not more than one-fifth of the available mind power.

The sub-conscious section of the mind operates automatically. It carries on all the necessary functions in connection with the building and the maintenance of the physical body; keeps the heart beating to circulate the blood; assimilates the food through a perfect system of chemistry, and delivers the food in liquid form throughout the body; removes worn out cells and replaces them with new cells; removes bacteria which are deleterious to health; creates new physical beings by the blending of the cells of protoplasm (the formative material of animal embryos) contributed by the male and female of living organisms.

These and many other essential functions are performed by the sub-conscious section of the mind, in addition to which *it serves as the connecting link between the conscious mind and Infinite Intelligence.*

It may be likened to the spigot of the conscious mind, through which (by its control through self-discipline) more thought power may be turned on. Or it may be likened to a rich garden spot wherein may be planted and germinated the seed of any desired idea.

The importance of the sub-conscious section of the mind may be estimated by recognition of the fact that it is the only means of *voluntary approach* to Infinite Intelligence. Therefore it is the medium by which all prayers are conveyed and all answers to prayer are received.

It is the medium that translates one's Definite Major Purpose into its material equivalent, *a process which consists entirely in guidance of the individual in the proper use of the natural means of attaining the objects of his desires.*

The sub-conscious section of the mind acts upon all impulses of thought, carrying out to their logical conclusion all thoughts which are definitely shaped by the conscious mind, *but it gives preference to thoughts inspired by emotional feeling,* such as the emotion of fear or the emotion of Faith; hence the necessity for self-discipline as a means of providing the sub-conscious mind with only those thoughts or desires which lead to the attainment of whatever one wishes.

The sub-conscious section of the mind gives preference also to the dominating thoughts of the mind—those thoughts which one creates by the repetition of ideas or desires. This fact explains the importance of adopting a Definite Major Purpose and the necessity of fixing that purpose (through self-discipline) as a dominating thought of the mind.

3. THE FACULTY OF WILL-POWER: The power of the will is the "boss" of all departments of the mind. It has the power to modify, change or balance all thinking habits, and its decisions are final and irrevocable except by itself. It is the power that puts the emotions of the heart under control, and it is subject to direction only by self-discipline. In this connection it may be likened to the Chairman of a Board of Directors whose decisions are final. It takes its orders from the conscious mind, *but recognizes no other authority.*

4. THE FACULTY OF REASON: This is the "presiding judge" of the conscious section of the mind which may pass judgment on all ideas, plans, and desires, and it will do so if it is directed by self-discipline. But its decisions can be set aside by the power of the will, or modified by the power of the emotions when the will does not interfere. Let us here take note of the fact that all accurate thinking requires the co-operation of the faculty of reason, *although it is a requirement which not more than one person in every ten thousand*

163

respects. This explains why there are so few accurate thinkers.

Most so-called thinking is the work of the emotions without the guiding influence of self-discipline; without relationship to either the power of the will or the faculty of reason.

5. THE FACULTY OF THE EMOTIONS: This is the source of most of the actions of the mind, the seat of most of the thoughts released by the conscious section of the mind. The emotions are tricky and undependable and may be very dangerous if they are not modified by the faculty of reason under the direction of the faculty of the will.

However, the faculty of the emotions is not to be condemned because of its undependability, for it is the source of all enthusiasm, imagination and Creative Vision, and it may be directed by self-discipline to the development of these essentials of individual achievement. The direction may be given by modification of the emotions through the faculties of the will and the reason.

Accurate thinking is not possible without complete mastery of the emotions.

Mastery is attained by placing the emotions under the control of the will, thus preparing them for direction to whatever ends the will may dictate, modifying them when necessary through the faculty of reason.

The accurate thinker has no opinions and makes no decisions which have not been submitted to, and passed upon by, the faculties of the will and the reason. He uses his emotions to *inspire the creation of ideas through his imagination*, but refines his ideas through his will and reason before their final acceptance.

This is self-discipline of the highest order. The procedure is simple but it is not easy to follow; and it is never followed except by the accurate thinker who moves on his own *personal initiative*.

The more important of the Twelve Riches, such as (1) a positive mental attitude, (2) harmony in human relationships, (3) freedom from fear, (4) the hope of achievement, (5) the capacity for faith, (6) an open mind on all subjects, and (7) sound physical health, *are attainable only by a strict direction and control of all the emotions*. This does not mean that the emotions should be suppressed, but they must be controlled and directed to definite ends.

164

The emotions may be likened to steam in a boiler, the power of which consists in its release and direction through the mechanism of an engine. Uncontrolled steam has no power, and though it be controlled it must be released through a governor, which is a mechanical device corresponding to self-discipline in connection with the control and release of emotional power.

The emotions which are most important and most dangerous are, (1) the emotion of sex, (2) the emotion of love, and (3) the emotion of fear. *These are the emotions which produce the major portion of all human activities.* The emotions of love and sex are creative. When controlled and directed they inspire one with imagination and creative vision of stupendous proportions. If they are not controlled and directed they may lead one to indulge in destructive follies.

6. THE FACULTY OF IMAGINATION: This is the workshop wherein are shaped and fashioned all desires, ideas, plans and purposes, together with the means of attaining them. Through organized use and self-discipline the imagination may be developed to the status of Creative Vision.

But the faculty of the imagination, like the faculty of the emotions, is tricky and undependable if it is not controlled and directed by self-discipline. Without control it often dissipates the power of thought in useless, impractical and destructive activities which need not be here mentioned in detail. *Uncontrolled imagination is the stuff that day dreams are made of!*

Control of the imagination begins with the adoption of definiteness of purpose based on definite plans. The control is completed by strict habits of self-discipline which give definite direction to the faculty of the emotions, for the power of the emotions is the power that inspires the imagination to action.

7. THE FACULTY OF THE CONSCIENCE: The conscience is the moral guide of the mind, and its major purpose is that of modifying the individual's aims and purposes so that they harmonize with the moral laws of nature and of mankind. The conscience is a twin-brother of the faculty of reason in that it gives discrimination and guidance to the reason when reason is in doubt.

The conscience functions as a co-operative guide only so long as it is respected and followed. If it is neglected, or its mandates are rejected, it finally becomes a conspirator instead of a guide, and often volunteers to justify man's most destructive habits. Thus the dual nature of the conscience makes it necessary for one to direct it through strict self-discipline.

8. THE SIXTH SENSE: This is the "broadcasting station" of the mind through which one automatically sends and receives the vibrations of thought. It is the medium through which all thought impulses known as "hunches" are received. And it is closely related to, or perhaps it may be a part of the sub-conscious section of the mind.

The sixth sense is the medium through which Creative Vision operates. It is the medium through which all basically new ideas are revealed. And it is the major asset of the minds of all men who are recognized as "geniuses."

9. THE MEMORY: This is the "filing cabinet" of the brain, wherein is stored all thought impulses, all experiences and all sensations that reach the brain through the five physical senses. And it may be the "filing cabinet" of all impulses of thought which reach the mind through the sixth sense, although all psychologists do not agree as to this.

The memory is tricky and undependable unless it is organized and directed by self-discipline.

10. THE FIVE PHYSICAL SENSES: These are the physical "arms" of the brain through which it contacts the external world and acquires information therefrom. The physical senses are not reliable, and therefore they need constant self-discipline. Under any kind of intense emotional activity the senses become confused and unreliable.

By the simplest sort of legerdemain the five physical senses may be deceived. And they are deceived daily by the common experiences of life. Under the emotion of fear the physical senses often create monstrous "ghosts" which have no existence except in the faculty of the imagination, and there is no fact of life which they will not and do not exaggerate or distort when fear prevails.

Control of Thought Habits

Thus we have briefly described the ten factors which enter into all mental activities of man. But we have supplied enough information concerning the "mechanism" of the mind to indicate clearly the necessity for self-discipline in their manipulation and use.

Self-discipline is attained by the control of thought habits. And the term "self-discipline" has reference only to the power of thought, because all discipline of self must take place in the mind, although its effects may deal with the functions of the physical body.

You are where you are and what you are because of your habits of thought!

Your thought habits are subject to your control!

They are the only circumstances of your life over which you have complete control, which is the most profound of all the facts of your life because it clearly proves that your Creator recognized the necessity of this great prerogative. Otherwise He would not have made it the sole circumstance over which man has been given exclusive control.

Further evidence of the Creator's desire to give man the unchallengeable right of control over his thought habits has been clearly revealed through the law of Cosmic Habitforce—the medium by which thought habits are fixed and made permanent, so that habits become automatic and operate without the voluntary effort of man.

For the present we are interested only in calling attention to the fact that the Creator of the marvelous mechanism known as a brain ingeniously provided it with a device by which all thought habits are taken over and given automatic expression.

Self-discipline is the principle by which one may voluntarily shape the patterns of thought to harmonize with his aims and purposes.

This privilege carries with it a heavy responsibility because it is the one privilege which determines, more than all others, the position in life which each man shall occupy.

If this privilege is neglected, by one's failure to voluntarily form habits designed to lead to the attainment of definite ends, *then the circumstances of life which are beyond one's control will do the job;* and what an extremely poor job it often becomes!

Every man is a bundle of habits. Some are of his own making while others are involuntary. They are made by his fears and doubts and worries and anxieties and greed and superstition and envy and hatred.

167

Self-discipline is the only means by which one's habits of thought may be controlled and directed until they are taken over and given automatic expression by the law of Cosmic Habitforce. Ponder this thought carefully, for it is the key to your mental, physical and spiritual destiny.

You can make your thought habits to order and they will carry you to the attainment of any desired goal within your reach. Or you can allow the *uncontrollable* circumstances of your life to make your thought habits for you and they will carry you irresistibly into the failure side of the great River of Life.

You can keep your mind trained on that which you desire from Life and get just that! Or you can feed it on thoughts of that which you *do not desire* and it will, as unerringly, bring you just that. *Your thought habits evolve from the food that your mind dwells upon.*

That is as certain as that night follows day!

Awake, arise, and quicken your mind to the attunement of the circumstances of life which your heart craves.

Turn on the full powers of your will and take complete control of your own mind. It is your mind! It was given to you as a servant to carry out your desires. And no one may enter it or influence it in the slightest degree *without your consent and co-operation*. What a profound fact this is!

Remember this when the circumstances over which you appear to have no control begin to move in and aggravate you. Remember it when fear and doubt and worry begin to park themselves in the spare bed-room of your mind. Remember it when the fear of poverty begins to park itself in the space of your mind that should be filled with a "prosperity consciousness."

And remember, too, that this is self-discipline! the one and only method by which anyone may take full possession of his own mind.

You are not a worm made to crawl in the dust of the earth.

If you were you would have been equipped with the physical means by which you would have crawled on your belly instead of walking on your two legs. Your physical body was designed to enable you to stand and to walk and to think your way to the highest attainment which you are capable of conceiving. Why be contented with less? Why should you insult

168

your Creator by indifference or neglect in the use of His most priceless gift—the power of your own mind?

Tap Your Inexhaustible Mind-Power

The potential powers of the human mind are beyond comprehension.

And one of the great mysteries which has endured down through the ages consists in man's neglect to recognize and to use these powers as a means of shaping his own earthly destiny!

The mind had been cleverly provided with a gateway of approach to Infinite Intelligence, through the subconscious section of the mind; and this gateway has been so arranged that it can be opened for voluntary use by preparation through that state of mind known as Faith.

The mind has been provided with a faculty of imagination wherein may be fashioned ways and means of translating hope and purpose into physical realities.

It has been provided with the stimulative capacity of desire and enthusiasm with which one's plans and purposes may be given action.

It has been provided with the power of the will through which both plan and purpose may be sustained indefinitely.

It has been given the capacity for Faith, through which the will and the reasoning faculty may be subdued while the entire machinery of the brain is turned over to the guiding force of Infinite Intelligence; and it has been prepared, through a sixth sense, for direct connection with other minds (under the Master Mind principle) from which it may add to its own power the stimulative forces of other minds which serve so effectively to stimulate the imagination.

It has been given the capacity to reason, through which facts and theories may be combined into hypotheses, ideas and plans.

It has been given the power to project itself into other minds, through what is known as telepathy.

It has been given the power of deduction by which it may foretell the future by analysis of the past. This capacity explains why the philosopher looks backward in order that he may see the future.

It has been provided with the means of selection, modification and control of the nature of its thoughts, thereby giving to man the privilege of building his own character to order, to fit any desired pattern, and the power to determine the kind of thoughts which shall dominate his mind.

It has been provided with a marvelous filing system for receiving, recording and recalling every thought it has expressed, through what is known as a memory, and this marvelous system automatically classifies and files related thoughts in such a manner that the recall of one particular thought leads to the recall of associated thoughts.

It has been provided with the power of emotion through which it can stimulate at will the body for any desired action.

It has been given the power to function secretly and silently, thereby insuring privacy of thought under all circumstances.

It has an unlimited capacity to receive, organize, store and express knowledge on all subjects, in both the fields of physics and metaphysics, the outer world and the *inner world*.

It has the power to aid in the maintenance of sound physical health, and apparently it is the sole source of cure of physical ills, all other sources being merely contributory; and it maintains a perfect repair system for the upkeep of the physical body—a system that works automatically.

It maintains and automatically operates a marvelous system of chemistry through which it converts food into suitable combinations for the maintenance and repair of the body.

It automatically operates the heart through which the blood stream distributes food to every portion of the body and removes all waste material and worn out cells of the body.

It has the power of self-discipline through which it can form any desired habit and maintain it until it is taken over by the law of Cosmic Habitforce and is given automatic expression.

It is the common meeting ground wherein man may commune with Infinite Intelligence, through prayer (or any form of expressed desire or definiteness of purpose) by the simple process of opening the gateway of approach through the subconscious section of the mind, by Faith.

It is the sole producer of every idea, every tool, every machine and every mechanical invention created by man for his convenience in the business of living in a material world.

It is the sole source of all happiness and all misery, and of both poverty and riches of every nature whatsoever, and it devotes its energies to the expression of whichever of these that dominates the mind through the power of thought.

It is the source of all human relationships, and all forms of intercourse between men; the builder of friendships and the creator of enemies, according to the manner in which it is directed.

It has the power to resist and defend itself against all external circumstances and conditions, although it cannot always control them.

It has no limitations within reason (no limitations except those which conflict with the laws of nature) save only those which the individual accepts through the lack of Faith! Truly, "whatever the mind can conceive and believe the mind can achieve."

It has the power to change from one mood to another at will. Therefore it need never be damaged beyond repair by any kind of discouragement.

It can relax into temporary oblivion through sleep, and prepare itself for a fresh start within a few hours.

It grows stronger and more dependable the more it is controlled, directed to definite ends and used voluntarily.

It can convert sound into music that rests and soothes both the body and the soul.

It can send the sound of the human voice around the earth in a fraction of a minute.

It can make two blades of grass grow where but one grew before.

It can build a printing press that receives a roll of paper at one end and turns out a completely printed and bound book at the other end, in a few moments.

It can call back the sunlight at will, at any time of the day, by merely causing the pushing of a button.

It can convert water into steam power and steam into electric power.

The mind can control the temperature of heat at will, and it can create fire by rubbing two sticks together.

It can produce music by drawing a hair from the tail of a horse across strings made from the internals of a cat.

It can accurately locate any position on earth by observation of the position of the stars.

It can harness the law of gravitation and make it do the work of man and beast in ways too numerous for mention.

It can build an airplane that will safely transport human beings through the air.

It can build a machine that will penetrate the human body with light and photograph the bones and the soft tissues without injury.

It has the power of clairvoyance through which it can discern physical objects not present or visible to the naked eye.

It can clear the jungle and convert the desert into a garden spot of productivity.

It can harness the waves of the oceans and convert them into power for the operation of machinery.

It can produce glass that will not break and convert wood pulp into clothing.

It can transform the stumbling-blocks of failure into stepping-stones of achievement.

It can build a machine that can detect falsehoods.

It can accurately measure any circle by the smallest fragment of its arc.

It can produce rubber from chemicals.

It can reproduce a picture of any material object, by television, without the aid of the human eye.

It can determine the size, weight and material contents of the sun, over 93,000,000 miles away, by analysis of the sun's rays of light.

It can create a mechanical eye that can detect the presence of airplanes or submarines, or any other physical object, hundreds of miles distant.

It can seal hermetically any type of food and preserve it indefinitely.

It can record and reproduce any sound, including the human voice, with the aid of a machine and a piece of wax.

It can record and reproduce pictures of any kind of physical motion, with the aid of a piece of glass and a strip of celluloid.

It can build a machine that will travel in the air, on the ground or under the water.

It can build a machine that will plough its way through the thickest forest, smashing trees as if they were cornstalks.

It can build a shovel that will lift as many tons of dirt in a minute as ten men could move in a day.

It can harness the magnetic poles of the northern and southern portions of the earth, with the aid of a compass, and determine direction accurately.

Great and powerful is the mind of man, and it shall yet perform feats which will make all the foregoing seem as trifles by comparison.

Negative Thoughts Lead to Self-destruction

And yet, despite all this astounding power of the mind the great majority of the people make no attempt to take control of their minds and they suffer themselves to become cowed by fears or difficulties which do not exist save in their own imaginations.

The arch enemy of mankind is fear!

We fear poverty in the midst of an over-abundance of riches!

We fear ill health despite the ingenious system nature has provided with which the physical body is automatically maintained, repaired and kept in working order.

We fear criticism when there are no critics save only those which we set up in our own minds through the negative use of our imagination.

We fear the loss of love of friends and relatives although we know well enough that our own conduct may be sufficient to maintain love through all ordinary circumstances of human relationship.

We fear old age whereas we should accept it as a medium of greater wisdom and understanding.

We fear the loss of liberty although we know that liberty is a matter of harmonious relationships with others.

We fear death when we know it is inevitable; therefore beyond our control.

We fear failure, not recognizing that every failure carries with it the seed of an equivalent benefit.

And we feared the lightning until Franklin and Edison and a few other rare individuals, who dared to take possession of their own minds, proved that lightning is a form of physical energy which can be harnessed and used for the benefit of mankind.

Instead of opening our minds for the guidance of Infinite

Intelligence, through Faith, we close our minds tightly with every conceivable shade and degree of self-imposed limitation based upon unnecessary fears.

We know that man is the master of every other living creature on this earth, yet we fail to look about us and learn from birds of the air and beasts of the jungle that even the dumb animals have been wisely provided with food and all the necessities of their existence through the universal plan which makes all fears groundless and foolish.

We complain of lack of opportunity and cry out against those who dare to take possession of their own minds, not recognizing that every man who has a sound mind has the right and the power to provide himself with every material thing he needs or can use.

We fear the discomfort of physical pain, not recognizing that pain is a universal language through which man is warned of evils and dangers that need correction.

Because of our fears we go to the Creator with prayers over petty details which we could and should settle for ourselves, then give up and lose Faith (if we had any Faith to begin with) when we do not get the results we ask for, not recognizing our duty to offer prayers of thanks for the bountiful blessings which we have been provided through the power of our minds.

We talk and preach sermons about sin, failing to recognize that the greatest of all sins is that of the loss of Faith in an all-wise Creator who has provided His children with more blessings than any earthly parent ever thinks of providing for his own children.

We convert the revelations of inventions into the tools of destruction through what we politely call "war," then cry out in protest when the law of compensation pays us off with famines and business depressions.

We abuse the power of the mind in ways too numerous for mention, because we have not recognized that this power can be harnessed through self-discipline, and used to serve our needs.

Thus we go all the way through life, eating the husks and throwing away the kernels of plenty!

The Art of Accurate Thinking

Before leaving the analysis of self-discipline, which deals entirely with the "mechanism" of thought, let us briefly describe some of the known facts and habits of thought in order that we may acquire the art of accurate thinking.

1. *All thought* (whether it is positive or negative, good or bad, accurate or inaccurate) *tends to clothe itself in its physical equivalent,* and it does so by inspiring one with ideas, plans, and the means of attaining desired ends, through logical and natural means.

After thought on any given subject becomes a habit and has been taken over by the law of Cosmic Habitforce, the subconscious section of the mind proceeds to carry it out to its logical conclusion, through the aid of whatever natural media that may be available.

It may not be literally true that "thoughts are things" but it is true that thoughts create all things, and the things they create are striking duplicates of the thought-patterns from which they are fashioned.

It is believed by some that every thought one releases starts an unending series of vibrations with which the one who releases the thought will later be compelled to contend; that man himself is but a physical reflection of thought put into motion and crystallized into physical form by Infinite Intelligence.

It is also the belief of many that the energy with which man thinks is but a projected minute portion of Infinite Intelligence, appropriated from the universal supply through the equipment of the brain. No thought contrary to this belief has yet been proved sound.

2. *Through the application of self-discipline* thought can be influenced, controlled and directed through transmutation to a desired end, by the development of voluntary habits suitable for the attainment of any given end.

3. *The power of thought* (through the aid of the subconscious section of the mind) *has control over every cell of the body,* carries on all repairs and replacements of injured or dead cells, stimulates their growth, influences the action of all

175

organs of the body and helps them to function by habit and orderliness, and assists in fighting disease through what is commonly called "body resistance." These functions are carried on automatically, but many of them may be stimulated by voluntary aid.

4. *All of man's achievements begin in the form of thought,* organized into plans, aims and purposes and expressed in terms of physical action. All action is inspired by one or more of the nine basic motives.

5. *The entire power of the mind* operates through two sections of the mind, the conscious and the sub-conscious.

The conscious section is under the control of the individual; the sub-conscious is controlled by Infinite Intelligence and serves as the medium of communication between Infinite Intelligence and the conscious mind.

The "sixth sense" is under the control of the sub-conscious section of the mind and it functions automatically in certain fixed fundamentals, but may be influenced to function in carrying out the instructions of the conscious mind.

6. *Both the conscious and the sub-conscious sections of the mind function in response to fixed habits,* adjusting themselves to whatever thought habits the individual may establish, whether the habits are voluntary or involuntary.

7. *The majority of all thoughts released by the individual are inaccurate* because they are inspired by personal opinions which are arrived at without the examination of facts, or because of bias, prejudice, fear, and the result of emotional excitement in which the faculty of the reason has been given little or no opportunity to modify them rationally.

8. *The first step in accurate thinking* (a step that is taken by none except those with adequate self-discipline) is that of separating facts from fiction and hearsay evidence. The second step is that of separating facts (after they have been identified as such) into two classes, viz.: important and the unimportant. An important fact is any fact which can be used to help one attain the object of his major purpose or any minor purpose leading to his major purpose.

All other facts are relatively unimportant. The average person spends his life in dealing with "inferences" based upon unreliable sources of information and unimportant facts. Therefore he seldom comes within sight of that form of self-discipline which demands facts and distinguishes the difference between important and unimportant facts.

9. *Desire, based on a definite motive, is the beginning of all voluntary thought action associated with individual achievement.*

The presence in the mind of any intense desire tends to stimulate the faculty of the imagination with the purpose of creating ways and means of attaining the object of the desire.

If the desire is continuously held in the mind (through the repetition of thought) it is picked up by the sub-conscious section of the mind and automatically carried out to its logical conclusion.

These are some of the more important of the known facts concerning the greatest of all mysteries, the mystery of human thought, and they indicate clearly that accurate thinking is attainable only by the strictest habits of self-discipline.

"Where," some may ask, "and how may one begin the development of self-discipline?"

It might well begin by *concentration* upon a Definite Major Purpose.

Nothing great has ever been achieved without the power of concentration.

How Self-Discipline May be Applied

The accompanying chart number one presents a complete description of the ten factors by which the power of thought is expressed. Six of these factors are subject to control through self-discipline, viz.:

1. The faculty of the will.
2. The faculty of the emotions.
3. The faculty of the reason.
4. The faculty of the imagination.
5. The faculty of the conscience.
6. The faculty of the memory.

The remaining four factors act independently, and they are not subject to voluntary control, except that the five physical senses may be influenced and directed by the formation of voluntary habits.

In chart number two we have presented a perspective picture which reveals the six departments of the mind over which self-discipline may be easily maintained.

CHART No. 1

CHART OF THE TEN FACTORS WHICH CONSTITUTE THE "MECHANISM" OF THOUGHT.
OBSERVE THAT THE SUBCONSCIOUS SECTION OF THE MIND
HAS ACCESS TO ALL DEPARTMENTS OF THE MIND.
BUT IS NOT UNDER THE CONTROL OF ANY.

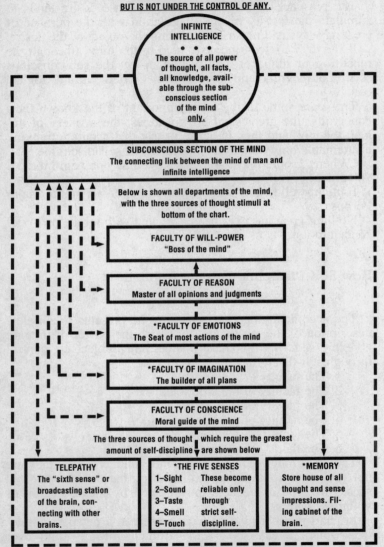

INFINITE INTELLIGENCE
• • •
The source of all power of thought, all facts, all knowledge, available through the subconscious section of the mind only.

SUBCONSCIOUS SECTION OF THE MIND
The connecting link between the mind of man and infinite intelligence

Below is shown all departments of the mind, with the three sources of thought stimuli at bottom of the chart.

FACULTY OF WILL-POWER
"Boss of the mind"

FACULTY OF REASON
Master of all opinions and judgments

*FACULTY OF EMOTIONS
The Seat of most actions of the mind

*FACULTY OF IMAGINATION
The builder of all plans

FACULTY OF CONSCIENCE
Moral guide of the mind

The three sources of thought which require the greatest amount of self-discipline are shown below

TELEPATHY
The "sixth sense" or broadcasting station of the brain, connecting with other brains.

*THE FIVE SENSES
1–Sight
2–Sound
3–Taste
4–Smell
5–Touch
These become reliable only through strict self-discipline.

*MEMORY
Store house of all thought and sense impressions. Filing cabinet of the brain.

*Not always dependable. Must be under strict discipline at all times.

178

CHART No. 2

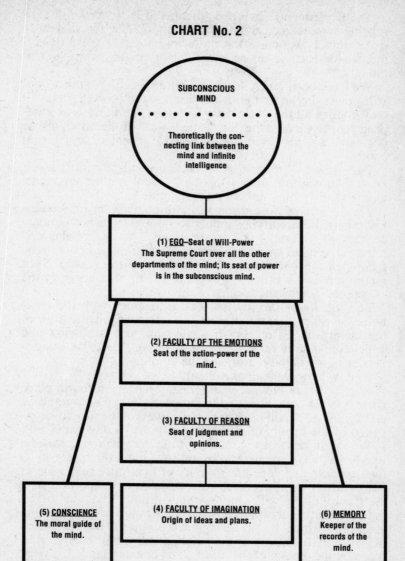

SUBCONSCIOUS MIND

Theoretically the connecting link between the mind and infinite intelligence

(1) EGO–Seat of Will-Power
The Supreme Court over all the other departments of the mind; its seat of power is in the subconscious mind.

(2) FACULTY OF THE EMOTIONS
Seat of the action-power of the mind.

(3) FACULTY OF REASON
Seat of judgment and opinions.

(5) CONSCIENCE
The moral guide of the mind.

(4) FACULTY OF IMAGINATION
Origin of ideas and plans.

(6) MEMORY
Keeper of the records of the mind.

CHART of THE SIX DEPARTMENTS of THE MIND over which
Self-discipline can be maintained, numbered in the order of their relative importance.

179

The departments have been numbered in the order of their relative importance, although it is impossible for anyone to say definitely which is the more important of these departments, for each is an essential factor in the expression of thought.

We have been given no choice but to place *ego*, the seat of will-power, in the first position, because the power of the will may control all the other departments of the mind, and it has been properly called the "Supreme Court" of the mind, whose decisions are final and not subject to appeal to any higher court.

The faculty of the emotions takes second position since it is well known that most people are ruled by their emotions; therefore, they rank next to the "Supreme Court."

The faculty of the reason takes third place in importance since it is the modifying influence through which emotional action may be prepared for safe usage. The "well balanced" mind is the mind which represents a compromise between the faculty of the emotions and the faculty of the reason. Such a compromise is usually brought about by the power of the "Supreme Court," the faculty of the will.

The faculty of the will sometimes decides with the emotions; at other times it throws its influence on the side of the faculty of reason, but it always has the last word, and whichever side it supports is the winning side of all controversies between the reason and the emotions.

And, what an ingenious system this is!

The faculty of the imagination has been given fourth place since it is the department which creates ideas, plans and ways and means of attaining desired objectives, all of which are inspired by the faculty of the emotions or the faculty of the will.

We might say that the faculty of the imagination serves the mind as a "ways and means committee," but it often acts on its own account and goes off on tours of fantastic exploration in places where it has no legitimate business in connection with the faculty of the will. On these self-inspired tours the imagination often has the full consent, cooperation and urge of the emotions, which is the main reason why all desires which originate in the faculty of the emotions must be closely scrutinized by the faculty of the reason; and countermanded, if need be, by the faculty of the will.

When the emotions and the imagination get out from under the supervision of the reason, and the control of the will, they resemble a couple of mischievous school boys who have decided to play hookey from school, and wind up at the old swimming hole, or in the neighbor's watermelon patch.

There is no form of mischief which these two may not get into! Therefore, they require more self-discipline than all the other faculties of the mind combined. Let us remember this!

The other two departments, the *conscience* and the *memory*, are necessary adjuncts of the mind, and while both are important they belong at the end of the list, where they have been assigned.

The subconscious section of the mind has been given the position above all of the other six departments of the mind because it is the connecting link between the conscious mind and Infinite Intelligence, and the medium through which all departments of the mind receive the power of thought.

The subconscious section of the mind is not subject to control, but it is subject to influence, by the means here described. It acts on its own accord, and voluntarily, although its action may be speeded up by intensifying the emotions, or applying the power of the will in a highly concentrated form.

A *burning desire* behind a Definite Major Purpose may stimulate the action of the subconscious section of the mind and speed up its operations.

The relationship between the subconscious section of the mind and the six other departments of the mind, indicated on chart number two, is similar in many respects to that of the farmer and the laws of nature through which his crops are grown.

The farmer has certain fixed duties to perform, such as preparing the soil, planting the seed at the right season, and keeping the weeds out, after which his work is finished. From there on out nature takes over, germinates the seed, develops it to maturity and yields a crop.

The conscious section of the mind may be compared with the farmer in that it prepares the way by the formulation of plans and purposes, under the direction of the faculty of the will. If this work is done properly, and a clear picture of that which is desired is created (the picture being the seed of the purpose desired) the subconscious takes over the picture, draws upon the power of Infinite Intelligence for the intelligence needed for the translation of the picture, gets the information necessary and presents it to the conscious section of the mind in the form of a practical plan of procedure.

Unlike the laws of nature which germinate seed and produce a crop for the farmer within a definite, predetermined length of time, the subconscious takes over the seed of ideas or purposes submitted to it and fixes its own time for the submission of a plan for their attainment.

Power of will, expressed in terms of a *burning desire*, is the one medium by which the action of the subconscious may be speeded up. Thus, by taking full possession of one's own mind, *by exercising the power of the will,* one comes into possession of power of stupendous proportions.

And the act of mastering the power of the will, so that it may be directed to the attainment of any desired end, is self-discipline of the highest order. Control of the will requires *persistence, faith and definiteness of purpose.*

In the field of salesmanship, for example, it is a fact well known to all master salesmen, that the persistent salesman heads the list in sales production. In some fields of selling, such as that of life insurance, persistence is the asset of major importance to the salesman.

And persistence, in selling or any other calling, is a matter of strict self-discipline!

In the field of advertising the same rule applies. The most successful advertisers carry on with unyielding persistence, repeating their efforts month after month, year after year, with unabating regularity; and professional advertising experts have convincing evidence that this is the only policy which will produce satisfactory results.

The pioneers who settled America when this country was only a vast wilderness of primitive men and wild animals, demonstrated what can be accomplished when will-power is applied with persistence.

At a later period in the history of our country, after the pioneers had established a semblance of civilized society, George Washington and his little army of under-fed, half-clothed, under-equipped soldiers proved once more that will-power applied with persistence is unbeatable.

And the pioneers of American industry gave us another demonstration of the benefits of will-power backed by persistence. Men of their type who have made great contributions to the American way of life were men with self-discipline,

182

and they attained it through the power of the will, backed with persistence.

Andrew Carnegie's entire career provides an excellent example of the benefits which are available through self-discipline. He came to America when he was a very young boy, and began work as a laborer. He had only a few friends; none of them wealthy or influential. But he did have an enormous capacity for the expression of his will-power.

By working at manual labor during the day and studying at night he learned telegraphy, and finally worked his way up to the position of private operator for the Division Superintendent of the Pennsylvania Railroad Company.

In this position he made such effective application of some of the principles of this philosophy, among them the principle of self-discipline, that he attracted the attention of men with money and influence who were in a position to aid him in carrying out the object of his Major Purpose in life.

At this point in his career he had precisely the same advantages that hundreds of other telegraph operators enjoyed, but no more. But he did have one asset which the other operators apparently did not possess: The will to win and a definite idea of what he wanted, together with persistence to carry on until he got it.

This too was the outgrowth of self-discipline!

Mr. Canegie's outstanding qualities were will-power and persistence, plus a strict self-discipline through which these traits were controlled and directed to the attainment of a definite purpose. Beyond these he had no outstanding qualities which are not possessed by the man of average intelligence.

Out of his will-power, properly self-disciplined and directed to the attainment of a definite purpose, came the great United States Steel Corporation which revolutionized the steel industry and provided employment for a huge army of skilled and unskilled workers.

Thus we see that *a successful man gets his start through the application of self-discipline, in pursuit of a definite purpose; and he carries on until he attains that purpose,* with the aid of that same principle.

Self-discipline is a self-acquired trait of character. It is not one which can be appropriated from the lives of others, nor acquired from the pages of a book. It is an asset which must come from *within*, by exercise of one's power of will. These self-acquired qualities are just as effective in other forms of application as they are in the attainment of leadership in industry.

When Andrew Carnegie said that "the power of will is an irresistible force which recognizes no such reality as failure," he doubtlessly meant that it is irresistible when it is properly organized and directed to a definite end in a spirit of faith. Obviously he intended to emphasize three important principles of this philosophy as the basis of all self-acquired self-discipline, viz.:

(a) Definiteness of Purpose.
(b) Applied Faith.
(c) Self-Discipline.

It should be remembered, however, that the state of mind which can be developed through these three principles can best be attained, and more quickly, by the application of other principles of this philosophy, among them:

(a) The Master Mind.
(b) A Pleasing Personality.
(c) The Habit of Going the Extra Mile.
(d) Personal Initiative.
(e) Creative Vision.

Combine these five principles with Definiteness of Purpose, Applied Faith and Self-Discipline, and you will have an available source of personal power of stupendous proportions.

The beginner in the study of this philosophy may find it difficult to gain control over his power of will without approaching that control step by step, through the mastery and application of these eight principles.

Mastery can be attained in one way only, and that is by constant, persistent application of the principles. They must be woven into one's daily habits and applied in all human relationships, and in the solution of all personal problems.

The power of the will responds only to *motive* persistently pursued!

And it becomes strong in the same way that one's arm may become strong—by systematic use.

Men with will-power which has been self-acquired, through self-discipline, do not give up hope or quit when the going becomes hard. Men without will-power do.

A humble general stood in review before an army of tired, discouraged soldiers who had just been badly defeated during

184

the War Between the States. He too had a reason to be discouraged, for the war was going against him.

When one of his officers suggested that the outlook seemed discouraging, General Grant lifted his weary head, closed his eyes, clenched his fists, and exclaimed: "We will fight it out along these lines if it takes all summer!" And he did fight it out along the lines he had chosen. Thus it may well be that on this firm decision of one man, backed by an indomitable will, came the final victory which preserved the union of the states.

One school of thought says that "right makes might!" Another school of thought says that "might makes right!" But men who think accurately know that the power of the will makes might, whether right or wrong, and the entire history of mankind backs up this belief.

Study men of great achievement, wherever you find them, and you will find evidence that the power of the will, organized and persistently applied, is the dominating factor in their success. Also, you will find that successful men commit themselves to a stricter system of self-discipline than any which is forced upon them by circumstances beyond their control.

They work when others sleep!

They Go the Extra Mile, and if need be another and still another mile, never stopping until they have contributed the utmost service of which they are capable.

Follow in their footsteps for a single day and you will be convinced that they need no taskmaster to drive them on. They move on their own personal initiative because they direct their efforts by the strictest sort of self-discipline.

They may appreciate commendation, but they do not require it to inspire them to action. They listen to condemnation, but they do not fear it, and they are not discouraged by it.

And they sometimes fail, or suffer temporary defeat, just as others do, but failure only spurs them on to greater effort.

They encounter obstacles, as does everyone, but these they convert into benefits through which they carry on toward their chosen goal.

They experience discouragements, the same as others do, but they close the doors of their minds tightly behind unpleasant experiences and transmute their disappointments into renewed energy with which they struggle ahead to victory.

When death strikes in their families they bury their dead, but not their indomitable wills.

They seek the counsel of others, extract from it that which they can use and reject the remainder, although the whole world may criticize them on account of their judgment.

They know they cannot control all the circumstances which affect their lives, but they do control *their own state of mind and their mental reactions* to all circumstances, by keeping their minds positive at all times.

They are tested by their own negative emotions, as are all people, but they keep the upper hand over these emotions by making right royal servants of them.

Let us keep in mind the fact that through self-discipline one may do two important things, both of which are essential for outstanding achievement.

First, one may completely control the negative emotions by transmuting them into constructive effort, using them as an inspiration to greater endeavor.

Secondly, one may stimulate the positive emotions, and direct them to the attainment of any desired end.

Thus, by controlling both the positive and the negative emotions the faculty of reason is left free to function, as is also the faculty of the imagination.

Control over the emotions is attained gradually, by the development of habits of thought which are conducive of control. Such habits should be formed in connection with the small, unimportant circumstances of life, for it is true, as Supreme Court Justice Brandeis once said, that "the brain is like the hand. It grows with use."

One by one the six departments of the mind which are subject to self-discipline can be brought under complete control, but the start should be made by habits which give one control over the emotions first, since it is true that most people are the victims of their uncontrolled emotions throughout their lives. Most people are the servants, not the masters of their emotions, because they have never established definite, systematic habits of control over them.

Every person who has made up his mind to control the six departments of his mind, through a strict system of self-discipline, should adopt and follow a definite plan to keep this purpose before him.

One student of this philosophy wrote a creed for this purpose, which he followed so closely that it soon enabled him to become thoroughly self-discipline conscious. It worked so successfully that it is here presented for the benefit of other students of the philosophy.

The creed was signed, and repeated orally, twice daily; once upon arising in the morning and once upon retiring at night. This procedure gave the student the benefit of the principle of auto-suggestion, through which the purpose of the creed was conveyed clearly to the subconscious section of his mind, where it was picked up and acted upon automatically.

The creed follows:

A CREED FOR SELF-DISCIPLINE!

Will-power:

Recognizing that the Power of Will is the Supreme Court over all other departments of my mind, I will exercise it daily, when I need the urge to action for any purpose; and I will form habits designed to bring the power of my will into action at least once daily.

Emotions:

Realizing that my emotions are both positive and negative I will form daily habits which will encourage the development of the positive emotions, and aid me in converting the negative emotions into some form of useful action.

Reason:

Recognizing that both my positive emotions and my negative emotions may be dangerous if they are not controlled and guided to desirable ends, I will submit all my desires, aims and purposes to my faculty of reason, and I will be guided by it in giving expression to these.

Imagination:

Recognizing the need for sound plans and ideas for the attainment of my desires, I will develop my imagination by calling upon it daily for help in the formation of my plans.

Conscience:

Recognizing that my emotions often err in their over-enthusiasm, and my faculty of reason often is without the warmth of feeling that is necessary to enable me to combine justice with mercy in my judgments, I will encourage my conscience to guide me as to what is right and what is wrong, *but I will never set aside the verdicts it renders,* no matter what may be the cost of carrying them out.

Memory:

Recognizing the value of an alert memory, I will encourage mine to become alert by taking care to impress it clearly with all thoughts I wish to recall, and by associating those thoughts with related subjects which I may call to mind frequently.

Subconscious Mind:

Recognizing the influence of my subconscious mind over my power of will, I shall take care to submit to it a clear and definite picture of my Major Purpose in life and all minor purposes leading to my major purpose, and I shall keep this picture constantly before my subconscious mind by repeating it daily.

Signed . . . .

Discipline over the mind is gained, little by little, by the formation of habits which one may control. Habits begin in the mind; therefore, a daily repetition of this creed will make one habit-conscious in connection with the particular kind of habits which are needed to develop and control the six departments of the mind.

The mere act of repeating the names of these departments has an important effect. It makes one conscious that these departments exist; that they are important; that they can be controlled by the formation of thought-habits; that the nature of these habits determines one's success or failure in the matter of self-discipline.

It is a great day in any person's life when he recognizes the fact that this success or failure throughout life is largely a matter of control over his emotions!

Before one can recognize this truth he must recognize the existence and the nature of his emotions, and the power which is available to those who control them—a form of recognition which many people never indulge in during their entire lifetime.

There is an alliance of men known as Alcoholics Anonymous, with a membership that spreads throughout the nation. These men operate in local Master Mind groups in almost

188

every city of the nation. And they are releasing one another from the evils of alcoholism on a scale which is nothing short of miraculous.

They operate entirely through self-discipline!

The medicine they use is the most powerful known to mankind. It consists of *the power of the human mind* directed to a definite end, that end being the end of alcoholism.

Here is an achievement which should inspire all men to become better acquainted with the power of their own minds. If the mind can cure alcoholism—and it is doing so—it can cure *poverty*, and *ill health*, and *fear*, and *self-imposed limitations!*

Alcoholics Anonymous is getting results because its members have been introduced to their "other selves"; those unseen entities which consist in the power of thought; the forces within the human mind which recognize no such reality as the "impossible."

This organization will live and it will grow, as all the forces of good must. The organization will eventually extend its service to include not only the elimination of the evils of alcoholism, but all other evils, such as the evils of fear, and poverty, and ill health, and hatred, and selfishness.

Eventually Alcoholics Anonymous will no doubt adopt the seventeen principles of this philosophy and provide its benefits for every member of that organization, as some of its members have already done with astounding effects.

It is a well known fact that *an enemy which has been recognized* is an enemy that is half defeated.

And this applies to enemies which operate within one's own mind as well as to those which operate outside of it; and especially does it apply to such enemies as negative emotions.

Once these enemies have been recognized one begins, almost unconsciously, to set up habits, through self-discipline, with which to counteract them.

This same reasoning applies also to the benefits of positive emotions, for it is true that a benefit recognized is a benefit easily utilized.

The positive emotions are beneficial, for they are a part of the driving force of the mind; but they are helpful only when they are organized and directed to the attainment of definite, constructive ends. If they are not so controlled they may be as dangerous as any of the negative emotions.

The medium of control is self-discipline, systematically and voluntarily applied through the habits of thought.

Take the emotion of Faith, for example:

This emotion, the most powerful of all the emotions, may be helpful only when it is expressed through constructive organized action based upon Definiteness of Purpose.

Faith without action is useless, because it may resolve itself into mere day-dreaming, wishing and faint hopefulness.

Self-discipline is the medium through which one may stimulate the emotion of Faith, through definiteness of purpose persistently applied.

The discipline should begin by establishing habits which stimulate the use of the power of the will, for it is the ego—the seat of the power of the will—in which one's desires originate. Thus, the emotions of Desire and Faith are definitely related.

Wherever a burning desire exists, there exists also the capacity for Faith which corresponds precisely with the intensity of the desire. The two are associated always. Stimulate one and you stimulate the other. Control and direct one, through organized habits, and you control and direct the other.

This is self-discipline of the highest order.

Benjamin Disraeli, believed by some to have been the greatest Prime Minister England ever had, attained that high station through the sheer power of his will, directed by Definiteness of Purpose.

He began his career as an author, but he was not highly successful in that field.

He published a dozen or more books, but none of them made any great impression on the public. Failing in this field he accepted his defeat as a challenge to greater effort in some other field—nothing more.

Then he entered politics, with his mind definitely set upon becoming the Prime Minister of the far-flung British Empire.

In 1837 he became a member of Parliament from Maidstone, but his first speech in Parliament was universally regarded as a flat failure.

Again he accepted his defeat as a challenge to try once more. Fighting on, with never a thought of quitting, he became the leader of the House of Commons by 1858, and later became the Chancellor of the Exchequer. In 1868 he realized his Definite Major Purpose by becoming the Prime Minister.

Here he met with terrific opposition (his "testing time" was at hand), which resulted in his resignation; but far from accepting his temporary defeat as failure, he staged a comeback and was elected Prime Minister a second time, after which he became a great builder of empires, and extended his influence in many different directions.

His greatest achievement perhaps was the acquisition of the Suez Canal—a feat which was destined to give the British Empire unprecedented economic advantages.

The keynote of his entire career was *self-discipline!*

In summarizing his achievements in one short sentence he said, "The secret of success is constancy of purpose!"

When the going was the hardest Disraeli turned on his willpower to its greatest capacity. It sustained him through the emergencies of temporary defeat, and brought him through to victory.

Here is the greatest of all the danger-points of the majority of men!

They give up and quit when the going becomes tough; and often they quit when *one more step* would have carried them triumphantly to victory.

Will-power is needed most when the oppositions of life are the greatest. And self-discipline will provide it for every such emergency, whether it be great or small.

The late Theodore Roosevelt was another example of what can happen when a man is motivated by the will to win despite great handicaps.

During his early youth he was seriously handicapped by chronic asthma and weak eyes. His friends despaired of his ever regaining his health, but he did not share their views, thanks to his recognition of the power of self-discipline.

He went West, joined a group of hard-hitting outdoor workers, and placed himself under a definite system of self-discipline, through which he built a strong body and a resolute mind. Some doctors said he could not do it—but he refused to accept their verdict.

In his battle to regain his health he acquired such perfect discipline over himself that he went back East, entered politics, and kept on driving until his will to win made him President of the United States.

Those who knew him best have said that his outstanding quality was a will which refused to accept defeat as anything more than an urge to greater effort. Beyond this his ability, his education, his experience were in no way superior to

191

similar qualities possessed by men all around him of whom the public heard little or nothing.

While he was President some army officials complained of an order he gave them to keep physically fit. To show that he knew what he was talking about he rode horseback a hundred miles, over rough Virginia roads, with the army officials trailing after him, trying hard to keep pace.

Behind all this physical action was an active mind which was determined not to be handicapped by physical weakness, and that mental activity reflected itself throughout his administration in the White House.

A French Expedition had tried to build the Panama Canal, but failed.

Theodore Roosevelt said "the canal shall be built" and he went to work then and there to express his faith in terms of action. The canal was built!

Personal power is wrapped up in the will to win!

But it can be released for action only by self-discipline, and by no other means.

Robert Louis Stevenson was a delicate youth from the day of his birth. His health prevented him from doing any steady work at his studies until he was past seventeen. At twenty-three his health became so bad that his physicians sent him away from England.

Then he met the woman of his choice and fell in love.

His love for her was so great that it gave him a new lease on life, a new motive for action, and he began to write, although his physical body was scarcely strong enough to carry him around. He kept on writing until he had greatly enriched the world by his writings, now universally accepted as masterpieces.

The same motive, love, has given the wings of thought to many another who, like Robert Louis Stevenson, has made this a richer and a better world. Without the motive of love Stevenson doubtless would have died without having made his contributions to mankind. He transmuted his love for the woman of his choice into literary works, through habits of self-discipline which placed the six departments of his mind under his control.

In a similar manner Charles Dickens converted a love tragedy into literary works which have enriched the world. Instead of going down under the blow of his disappointment

192

in his first love affair, he drowned his sorrow through the intensity of his action in writing. In that manner he closed the door behind an experience which many another might have used as a door of escape from his duty—an alibi for his failure.

Through self-discipline he converted his greatest sorrow into his greatest asset, for it revealed to him the presence of that "other self" wherein consisted the power of genius which he reflected in his literary works.

There is one unbeatable rule for the mastery of sorrows and disappointments, and that is transmutation of those emotional frustrations, through definitely planned work. It is a rule which has no equal.

And the secret of its power is self-discipline.

Freedom of body and mind, independence, and economic security are the results of personal initiative expressed through self-discipline. By no other means may these universal desires be assured.

You must travel the remainder of the distance alone. If you have followed the instructions I have given you, in the right kind of mental attitude, you are now in possession of the great Master-Key.

Now I shall reveal to you a great truth of the utmost importance: The Master-Key to Riches consists entirely in the greatest power known to man; the power of thought!

You may take full possession of the Master-Key by taking possession of your own mind, through the strictest of self-discipline.

Through self-discipline you may *think* yourself into or out of any circumstances of life!

Self-discipline will help you to control your mental attitude. Your mental attitude may help you to master every circumstance of your life, and to convert every adversity, every defeat, every failure into an asset of equivalent scope. That is why a Positive Mental Attitude heads the entire list of the Twelve Riches of Life.

Therefore, it should be obvious to you that the great Master-Key to Riches is nothing more nor less than the self-discipline necessary to help you take full and complete possession of your own mind!

Start right where you stand, and become the master of yourself. Start now! Be done forever with that old self which

193

has kept you in misery and want. Recognize and embrace that "other self" which can give you everything your heart craves.

Remember it is profoundly significant that the only thing over which you have complete control is your own mental attitude!

For this is the Master-Key to Riches!

Upon request, the owner of this book may receive an autographed bookplate bearing the signature of the author. Address your request to The Napoleon Hill Foundation, 1440 Paddock Drive, Northbrook, IL 60062, enclosing a large, self-addressed, stamped envelope. With this bookplate you will receive a copy of one of Dr. Hill's famous success essays.

ABOUT THE AUTHOR

NAPOLEON HILL began at an early age to study great achievers such as Andrew Carnegie, Thomas Edison, and Alexander Graham Bell. He became the world's foremost scholar and thinker in the science of human success and the author of *Think and Grow Rich, You Can Work Your Own Miracles, The Master-Key to Riches, Grow Rich! With Peace of Mind*, and, with E. Harold Keown, *Succeed and Grow Rich Through Persuasion*. After Hill's death his unfinished work was completed by Dennis Kimbro as *Think and Grow Rich: A Black Choice*.